The Pleasures
of Railways

A JOURNEY BY TRAIN

THROUGH THE DELECTABLE COUNTRY

OF ENTHUSIASM FOR

RAILWAYS

Brian Hollingsworth

PENGUIN BOOKS

Penguin Books Ltd, Harmondsworth, Middlesex, England
Penguin Books, 40 West 23rd Street, New York, New York 10010, U.S.A.
Penguin Books Australia Ltd, Ringwood, Victoria, Australia
Penguin Books Canada Ltd, 2801 John Street, Markham, Ontario, Canada L3R 1B4
Penguin Books (N.Z.) Ltd, 182–190 Wairau Road, Auckland 10, New Zealand

First published by Allen Lane 1983
Published in Penguin Books 1984

Made and printed in Great Britain by
Richard Clay (The Chaucer Press) Ltd,
Bungay Suffolk
Set in Monophoto Ehrhardt 10 on 13 pt

PENGUIN BOOKS

THE PLEASURES OF RAILWAYS

Brian Hollingsworth had formed an extravagant passion for railways even before he can remember. Since then a career as an engineer with the Great Western Railway and British Railways as well as indulgence in most of the manifestations of amateur railway enthusiasts has done nothing to blunt it.

Since leaving BR in 1974 he has written a number of books bearing on the subject of railways, but maintains first-hand contact with the industry by being a director of the Romney, Hythe and Dymchurch Railway and by advising the Ffestiniog Railway on civil-engineering matters. As well as writing about railways, his activities include the building of his own one-fifth full-size Groesor Junction and Pacific Railway in the mountains of Wales. Brian Hollingsworth's other publications are *Steam into the Seventies, Steam for Pleasure, North American Railways, How to Drive a Steam Locomotive* (Penguin), *Atlas of the World's Railways, An Atlas of Train Travel, Ffestiniog Adventure, Great Western Adventure, Model Railways, Illustrated Encyclopaedia of the Steam Passenger Locomotive* and *'LBSC' – His Life and Locomotive*.

CONTENTS

LIST OF PLATES

I · INTRODUCTION

Not in vain the distance beckons.
Forward, forward let us range,
Let the great world spin for ever
Down the ringing grooves of change.

ALFRED LORD TENNYSON, *Locksley Hall*
(*Tennyson was short-sighted and although present
at the opening of the Liverpool & Manchester
Railway, thought that the trains ran in grooves
not on rails*)

The railways of the world are severely practical things built for the mundane purpose of taking goods and people from one place to another. But to many members of the human race they have another role, as instruments of pleasure, the entertainment staged upon their tracks being as absorbing to their *aficionados* as, for example, a great symphony performed by some famous orchestra.

This book is intended to put before its readers the many different ways in which the lovers of railways extract pleasure from objects of their affection. The main story is told in the form of a railway journey which takes an aspirant across the whole field of enjoyment of railways, beginning with the pleasure of looking up the trains in the timetable.

Much is made of the What, How, When and Where of finding pleasure from railways; the problem, of course, lies in the Why – the question 'Why do railways provide enjoyment?' To this question the book as a whole must be regarded as an attempt to give some sort of answer, inadequate though it may be.

But even if one cannot solve with any certainty the mystery of the iron road's magnetism, one can at least say something about the different roles that people can play when enjoying the railway hobby.

The roles available begin with the relatively passive one of spectator – someone who just likes to watch the trains go by – and end with the entirely positive one of re-creator, whether of models or of full-size trains. Of course, there is no reason why one should not perform in several of the roles at once. More than that, it is often desirable. Take someone who perhaps sets out to be a re-creator in miniature of, say, the old London & South Western Railway. It is obviously better if he is, or becomes, an expert in its nuts-and-bolts as well. On the other hand, one can know how many cylinder-head bolts there were on some rare and long-forgotten railway locomotive without having to make a model of it; and one can make a good model of that or any similar rarity by using published drawings – or even perhaps a manufactured kit – without necessarily being an expert. But in salute to those whose dedication makes it all possible, pride of place goes to the role of professional railwayman, to cover those who not only love their railway but also marry it.

There can be few industries which include amongst their staff such a high percentage of people for whom going to work is just another opportunity to indulge their favourite pastime, and who go home after nearly every shift secure in the knowledge that they have earned real folding money just by doing what they like doing best. But before speaking of railway jobs which people like, it must be recognized that amongst them are some that are not, and were not, enjoyed. One might read about a few in *Life in a Railway Factory* by Alfred Williams (1915, reprinted David & Charles 1969). In another part of the forest, this writer (who admits he enjoyed most of the jobs he did in twenty-eight years on British Railways) once had to arrange for the Chairman to attend a certain event then long in the future. Warned that one had to ask in good time, he found that, six months ahead of the week in question, the great man already had every morning, evening and all but two afternoons booked. Those at the very top find themselves prisoners of their own importance.

On the other hand, many lesser but freer railwaymen also feel their work is their life. For example, in the days before mechanization changed things, each few miles of railway was looked after by a small group of men known as a length gang. In charge of each group was a ganger, who took personal responsibility for the safe running of trains over his length. In this respect, of course, he was more important than the Chairman. A typical ganger's attitude of mind is summed up by a conversation that took place regarding the edging of the ballast by stones which were being laid out with a straight edge. Someone asked, 'Is such extra trouble worthwhile?' The answer – 'Every picture needs a frame, sir' – put the quite important questioner nicely in his place.

A word of thanks is due also to another group of those who make possible the existence of this amazing worldwide railway network which we love so much. These are the railway users – the travellers, in fact, who use railways because they have to, or find it best to, but not because they like to. And with travellers must be coupled the customers who enable railways to exist by sending their freight that way.

Just as railwaymen are divided into railway-lovers and others, amongst the railway customers can be found a proportion of train-lovers. Of the latter some just enjoy rail travel; others collect journeys over an ever increasing proportion of the world's million miles of railways. A chemist from Wolverhampton, England, called Perkins was famous for travelling every mile of 20,000 miles plus of railway in the British Isles, between 1900 and 1950.

A witty account of the extension of Perkins' feat to the whole world, based on its author's exploits, comes in *All Aboard with E. M. Frimbo* by Rogers Whitaker and Anthony Hiss (André Deutsch, 1975). While on the subject of books on rail travel, this author, long motivated by a period spent in the back rooms of the aircraft industry into thinking that steel wheels firmly set on steel rails form the basis of the best way to move around, has recently set out the possibilities and the problems in *An Atlas of Train Travel* (Excalibur Books, 1980).

We now turn from those who merely run or use railways to those who worship them. The most usual way of paying homage to any deity is to record its manifestations, and in this the worship of railways is no exception. From the schoolboy spotter who writes engine numbers and names in a notebook at his local station to the photographer who flies round the world with a festoon of expensive cameras and tape-recorders round his neck, we all do it. Firms like Kodak and Ilford have great reason to bless the latter, while publishers like David & Charles and Ian Allan owe their worldwide businesses to the former. Ian Allan began trading after his Southern Railway boss turned down the idea of an official printed spotters' list of engine numbers. Ian's unofficial printed list led in due time to an occasion when he entertained the Southern Region Board to lunch in his own Pullman Car-cum-Boardroom at Shepperton. Of course, when recording engine numbers palls, one can proceed to carriage and even wagon numbers, while maturity brings such black magic as the pentacle-like lines of track layout plans.

An elite group amongst the recorders are the martyrs – those who have been imprisoned for their work. A friend of the writer, a few years ago, spent several days as the guest of the Polish government, making the front page of several national daily newspapers, as a result of scribbling down engine numbers in a notebook, and many others, while not going so far as staying overnight, have also spent time 'inside'. In this way train-spotting and train-photting (a regrettable new word now appearing in the vocabulary of 'gricing') is made an even more exciting and worthwhile pastime.

Another aspect of this recording-worship recognizes that the art-form of railways involves movement; so one writes down, to the nearest tenth of a second, the time at which one's train passes every station, signal box and gradient change on its route. Books, far too numerous to list, have been filled with these strange votive offerings, which, alas, are to the unconverted somewhat dull, although to their devotees the art of train-timing is all-absorbing.

As with other forms of religious observance, the drawback is that the form becomes an end in itself when carried to extremes, thereby obscuring the wonders of a creation that well deserves all the homage paid to it and more.

Not all the recorders of the world's railways let the matter rest there: some go on to become experts in some particular facet. On our railway journey to come, they are the people who will sit by our side and explain all the wonders to be seen as we encounter them. Just mention an engine number and the right expert will instantly tell us who designed her, who built her and when, not to speak of her nuts-and-bolts, from wheel diameter to type of injector. Like Kipling's Elephant's Child, we are all stoked full of ''satiable curtiosity'; so, even if we sometimes regard experts in the light of bi-coloured python rock snakes ('they always talk like that', if you remember), it is nice sometimes to know why – for example – French trains always keep to the left-hand track except in the province of Alsace-Lorraine, or why some Italian steam locomotives have chimneys at the side rather than up at the front. It would take more than an expert, though, to say why square ones were used on old Belgian engines.

British Railways became painfully aware of these knowledge-able amateurs on the occasion of the funeral of His Majesty King George VI. The 'Royal' locomotive *Windsor Castle* was under repair in the shops, so the name and number plates were trans-ferred to another of the same class. The protests of the experts who easily spotted the minor differences between two nominally identical locomotives made the national press next day.

The paraphernalia of railways has not escaped attention from those who have squirrel-like instincts. It is quite common now to see the number plate that once identified a hard-working steam locomotive adorning the walls of an elegant drawing room. As a measure of how things have moved, name plates that were once a drug on the market at £2 now change hands for four-figure sums.

Single-line signalling tokens, telephone and telegraph insulator 'dollies', crockery and cutlery, posters, block-bells, locomotive speedometers, gradient posts, 'Trespassers William' signs and much else besides have now an antique-shop rather than a scrap value. And as with other kinds of antiques, 'reproduction' items are available for many of these things. In Britain, our national railways are now fully alive to the existence in this field of an antique-collecting market and they channel their own relics into it via their famous Collectors' Corner, adjacent to Euston Station, London.

The world's railway systems are changing faster than most enthusiasts like; but since most of us who mind have heard of King Canute, our hopes and dreams lie in re-creating the old ways rather than trying to stem the tide of progress.

The weight of artifact involved in this process of re-creation runs downwards from a Union Pacific Railroad 485-ton 'Challenger' 4–6–6–4; while the greatest length of restored track is in the nearby Rockies, on the Cumbres & Toltec Scenic Railroad's eighty-six miles of mountain and desert railway between Chama, New Mexico, and Antonito, Colorado. At the same time the gauge between the rails ranges from 7 feet o$\frac{1}{4}$ inch – for broad-gauge trackage currently being laid at the Great Western Society's depot at Didcot – to about $\frac{1}{4}$ inch – the gauge of 'Miniclub' commercial model trains made by Maerklin of West Germany.

2 · THE ART OF TIMETABLING

Yet there isn't a train I wouldn't take,
no matter where it's going.

EDNA ST VINCENT MILLAY

The first step in taking any railway journey is to consult the timetable. At once we are in contact with one of the most subtle and seductive of all forms of railway art, and – as all art-forms should be – occasionally the most exasperating.

A salute is due first to that greatest of timetable artists, the firm of Thomas Cook, who offer the world's trains in their *Continental and Overseas Timetables of Railway, Bus and Steamer Services*. Amongst their many virtues is that clarity is not lost in spite of compressing, for example, most of Britain into fifty-two $6\frac{1}{2}$ by $9\frac{1}{2}$ inch sheets. British Railways own timetable needs 1,160 similar sheets to say what is effectively the same thing, covering only some 10 per cent more in terms of passenger journeys. The oddest feature of the case is that B.R. used to own Thomas Cook but never used the latter firm's expertise to produce a handy timetable. All strength to B.R., though, in doing its own thing. Hence Britain's national timetable is a superb and quite different manifestation of this branch of railway art, in that it pursues absolute completeness and logicality to the end, quite regardless of economy and convenience.

Nearly all (you may be surprised to learn that it is not quite all) the world's 500 or so railway administrations which provide passenger service do produce a public timetable; in many cases where there are separate administrations in one country, a national timetable is produced. In some countries, buses, steamers and ropeways might also be included.

All the best timetables (best from the artistic point of view, that is) are covered in obscure pointing hands and insignificant footnotes in very small print which say such things as 'runs alternate Mondays only', so that looking up a train in them is not only an art but also an adventure.

Of course, timetables are not only of use (with an unusually closely specified period for remaining in fashion) but, like other *objets d'art*, also things to collect and to enjoy. If this book was a game of snakes and ladders, one is now at a ladder (or snake) leading to Chapter 24, 'The End of the Line'; this is because for many people timetables are the be-all and end-all. Why bother with all the tedium of travel when a few back numbers of Bradshaw, the *Official Guide*, the *Indicateur Chaix* and a few others can transport one into a wonderful world of planning a trip from, say, Hollingsworth, Louisiana, U.S.A., to Medicine Hat, Alberta, Canada?

When arranging a collection of timetables on one's library shelves – a difficult task when they vary from a tiny single sheet to volumes the size of *Encyclopaedia Britannica* – one might even have doubts how to classify them. It has been known for unkind people in sarcastic mood to refer to railway timetables as works of fiction, and just occasionally one does find pages which this cap fits. For example, the elegant sheet reproduced herewith, showing what was supposed to happen in South Devon on summer Saturday afternoons of long ago, was really only of aesthetic value – there were just not enough tracks to run all these trains. Even so, the arrangement is an example of the highest flights of the timetabler's art. Lest one should be misunderstood, turn the page from 'Saturdays Only' to 'Mondays to Fridays' and the fiction jibe no longer applies; those pages held promises that were almost always kept even in those high and far-off pre-war days. Notice the delightful nomenclature, with such information as 'Restaurant Car Train' printed in full in the column.

SATURDAYS ONLY —continued.

	a.m.	a.m.	a.m.	a.m.	a.m.	a.m.	a.m.	a.m.	noon	noon	p.m.	p.m.	a.m.	a.m.	p.m.	p.m.	a.m.
LONDON (Paddington) dep.			8 50	7 30			9 0	9 30		1025		10 30		1035	1040			1050
Reading "				8 14			9 50											
Oxford "							9E5											
Bath "		8 37		9 51														
Bristol (Temple Meads) "		8 56		10 7														
Manchester (L'nd'n Rd) dep.																		
Liverpool { Land St'ge																		
{ Lime Street																		
Birkenhead (Woodside) "																		
Chester "																		
Crewe "																		
Bristol (Temple Meads) arr.																		
Wolverhampton (L.L.) dep.				A10			8 10									9 0		
Birmingham (Snow Hill) "				A10												9 40		
Bristol (Temple Meads) arr.				10A9														
Fishguard Harbour dep.				5 10														
Swansea (High Street) "				7 0														
Cardiff (General) "				8 43														
Newport "				9 5														
Bristol (Temple Meads) arr.				9 55														
BRISTOL (T'ple M'ds) dep.		9 5		10 15		10E25												
arr.		10 29		11 13		11 50	11 45											
TAUNTON dep.			1035	1050	11 18	11 28	1140	1147		1155			1217			12 30	1255	
Norton Fitzwarren "			10 40	10 54	11 34													
Wellington "			1052			11 45					12 0				12 42			
Burlescombe "			11 2	STOP					STOP						STOP			
Sampford Peverell "			11 7								12 30							
Tiverton Junction "			11 14			12 18					12 36							
Tiverton (M) arr.			11 42			12 47					12 47							
Cullompton dep.			11 18								12 36							
Hele and Bradninch "			11 26								12 36							
Silverton "			11 30								12 43							
Stoke Canon "			11 36								12 55							
EXETER { St. David's dep.			11 45			11 56		12 20	12 45		12 55	1 28			1 55	1 55		
{ St. Thomas dep.			11 25	1152		12 2		1230	12 45		12 59	1 33		1 40		1 40		
Exminster "			11 36	12 3							1 3							
Starcross (for Exmouth) "			11 43	12 10							1 44							
Dawlish Warren "			11 56	12 15							1 50							
Dawlish "			11 55															
Teignmouth "			11 3		1215	12 25		1 2	1 10									
Newton Abbot arr.			12 15	12 35		12 45		1 12	1 20									
Bovey { M arr.	1 1			1 27		1 22												
Moretonhampstead "	1 25			1 55	1 22			2 30		2 30								
Torre arr.	12 33			12 40	12 57			1 43										
Torquay "	12 36			12 50	12 57		1 20	1 43										
Paignton "	12 44			1 0	1 10		1 24	1 55										
Brixham (M) "	1 7			1 25	1 39													
Kingswear "	1 7			1 25	1 42			2 41										
Dartmouth "	1 26		p.m.	1 55	1 52 p.m			2 47										
Newton Abbot dep.	STOP		12 20		STOP	12 45												
Totnes "			12 35			1 16												
Brent "			12 51			1 16		1 28										
Kingsbridge arr.			W65			5 5		2 55										
Salcombe (W. Natl. Bus) "			W65			5 5												
Wrangaton dep.			11 55															
Bittaford Platform "			12 59															
Ivybridge "			1 3															
Cornwood "			1 8															
Plympton "			1 15															
{ North Rd. arr.	p.m.		1 20					1 50				2 47			3 15	3 15		
PLYMOUTH { Millbay "	1 15			p.m.	1 45			1 55			2040	2 55			3 05	3 26		
{ North Rd. dep.								2 5			2040	255			3 26			
Devonport "			1 21		1 50			2 10										
Dockyard Halt "					1 55			2 14										
Ford Halt "					1 54			2 14										
Keyham "			1 24		1 56			2 17										
St. Budeaux Platform "					1 59			2 21										
Saltash (for Callington) "			1 30		2 3													
St. Germans "			1 40															
Menheniot "			1 50															
Liskeard "			1 59															
Looe arr.			3 35												3 53			
Doublebois dep.			2 6												4 45			
Bodmin Road "			2 15															
Bodmin arr.			2 50												4 9			
Wadebridge "			3 12												4 48			
Padstow (Southern Rly.) "			3 36												5 10			
Lostwithiel dep.			2 24												5 36			
Fowey (M) arr.			2 55									3 40						
Par dep.			2 34									4 15			4 22			
Newquay arr.															5 20			
St. Austell dep.			2 45								3 37				5 20			
Grampound Road "			2 57												4 34			
Probus and Ladock Platform "			3 4								4 40							
Truro arr.			3 10												4 58			
FALMOUTH arr.			4 20															
Truro dep.			3 15					3 20				5 T10	5 10		9 50			
Chacewater "			3 25					3 5							5 0			
Scorrier "			3 30															
Redruth "			3 37												5 10			
Carn Brea "			3 41															
Camborne "			3 47															
Gwinear Road "			3 52								4 45							
Helston arr.			5 15								5 15							
The Lizard (W. Natl. Bus) "			6J20								6J20							
Hayle dep.			4 3												5 36			
St. Erth "			4 10															
St. Ives arr.			4 46							4 41					5 55			
Marazion "			4 20							5 5					5 55			
PENZANCE arr.			4 30								4 55	5 10			5 50			
Land's End (W. Natl. Bus) arr.			6 10								6 10				7 5			

A — Applies Sept. 16th and 23rd only. Through carriages to Torquay and Paignton.   **B** — Via Birmingham and Stratford-on-Avon.
D — Change at Devonport.   **E** — Via Reading. Slip carriage to Reading.
F — Bristol (Stapleton Road).   **H** — Liverpool Central (Low Level) via Birmingham and Stratford-on-Avon.

J — On September 16th and 23rd, dep. 9.5 a.m.
K — Commencing Sept. 2nd, arrive 3.25 p.m.
L — Commencing Sept. 2nd, calls Truro at 5.25 p.m.
M — One class only.
N — On Sept. 16th and 23rd, calls Taunton at 3.2 p.m. to set down only.

THE TIMES ON THIS PAGE APPLY SATURDAYS ONLY.

For Service MONDAYS to FRIDAYS see pages 86 to 88A.

Out of sight (in theory at least) to all but professional railway-men is the working timetable. Again a summer Saturday page is reproduced. The year is not the same, so the times are not quite the same either, but we are still in the realms of fiction. Notice that some times are specified to the nearest half-minute, when in real life even half-hour delays were a counsel of perfection seldom achieved.

Other railways use an elegant graphical working timetable which vividly shows the operation of trains over a section of line. Places and distance are shown vertically, while the lapse of time is shown horizontally. The movement of individual trains in space and time are shown by diagonal lines; the steeper the line the faster the train. Information which needs a whole book to describe in conventional form can be set down graphically on only a few sheets. Alas, a fear that engineers might take them over has deterred operators of railways in Britain from adopting such an excellent arrangement.

The working timetable for British Railways is a shelf-full of volumes – even a set of freight timetables alone is far too heavy to carry around. Not all railways are run this way; this writer had the pleasure of being present at 1 Market Street, San Francisco, when the Chief Operating Officer of B.R. asked if he could see the Southern Pacific Railroad's working timetables. Naturally expecting an armful of hefty books, his expression when a single sheet of paper covering the whole 12,000-mile system was produced would have ensured his success down the coast in Hollywood. S.P. run all but a few of their trains on an 'as required' basis!

Like icebergs which maintain seven-eighths of their beautiful shapes out of sight below the water, there is much more yet. Even some railroads outside North America run most of their trains 'as required', but most of the rest of the world backs up its working timetables with many other documents. Returning again to summer Saturdays in Devon, for example, there is a programme of carriage workings showing how the trains which

Up Trains.

STATIONS.	A Crewe Passenger.		11.50 a.m. Exmouth Jct. to Friary South'n 'm Frght	H 4.20 a.m. Laira to Severn Tunnel Junction Freight.		A 8.15 a.m. Perranporth Passenger SO		A Wolverhampton Passenger. SO		A Nottingham Passenger. SO	
	arr.	dep.	dep.	arr.	dep.	arr.	dep.	arr.	dep.	arr.	dep.
	a.m.	a.m.	p.m.	a.m.	a.m.	a.m.	a.m.	a.m.	a.m.	a.m.	a.m.
Penzance	—	7 40	RR	—	—	....	....	—	7 30	..	..
Plymouth	10 17	10 26		—	4 20	10 38		10 24	10 33	..	..
Ashburton Jct. ←–■	11	7	....	6 32		11 26		11 11		....	
Dainton Siding ...	—	—	....	—	—	—	—	—	—	....	
Stop Brd. 217m.57c.	—	—	..	6 45	P6 49	—	—	—	—	....	
Stoneycombe Siding	—	—	..	—	—	—	—	—	—	....	
KINGSWEAR	..	..	..	..	..						
Kingswear C'sing	..	..	..	..	..						
Churston	....	....	..	..	..	SUS	PEN	SUS	PEN	SUS	PEN
Stop Bd. 10½ m.p.	..	..	..	..	..	DE	D	DE	D	DE	D
Goodrington S. H.	....	..	..	..	..	....		....		....	
Goodrington Yard	..	..	..	..	..						
Paignton	..	..	..	..	..			—		—	11 5
Gas House Siding	..	..	..	..	..					—	—
TORQUAY	..	..	..	..	..					11 10	11 15
Torre	..	..	..	..	..					—	—
Kingskerswell	..	..	..	..	..					—	—
Aller Junction	11	19		6 59	P7 3	11 38		11 23		11 27	
NEWTON ABBOT	11 21	11 29		7	7	11 40	Q11 44	11 25	11 32	11 30	11 37
Hackney	—	—		7 9E	T7 38	—	—	—	—	—	—
Old Quay	—	—		—	—	—	—	—	—	—	—
Teignmouth	—	—		—	—	—	—	—	—	—	—
Dawlish	—	—		—	—	—	—	—	—	—	—
Dawlish Warren	—	—		—	—	—	—	—	—	—	—
Starcross	—	—		—	—	—	—	—	—	—	—
Exminster	—	—		8 16	* 8 48	—	—	—	—	—	—
City Basin Jct.	—	—		—	—	—	—	—	—	—	—
St. Thomas	—	—		—	—	—	—	—	—	—	—
EXETER (St. David's)	11 55	12 3	12 6	—	—	12 10		12 0		12 5	●1213
Exeter (Riverside)	—	—		9 2	9 40	—	—	—	—	—	—
Cowley Bridge Jct.	12	6	12 10	—	—	12 12		12 3		12 16	
Stoke Canon	—	—		—	—	—	—	—	—	—	—
Silverton	—	—	....	—	—	—	—				
Hele and Bradninch	—	—	....	10 1	*11 22	—	—	5 minutes		2 minutes	
Cullompton	—	—	....	—	—	—	—	recovery		recovery	
Tiverton Junction	—	—	....	—	—	—	—	Exeter to		Exeter to	
Sampford Peverell	—	—	....	—	—	—	—	Whiteball		Whiteball.	
Burlescombe	—	—	....	—	—	—	—				
Whiteball Tunnel	12	29	....	11	57	12 36		12 30		12 41	
Wellington (Som.)	—	—	....	—	—	—	—				
Poole Siding	—	—	....	—	—	—	—				
Victory Siding	—	—	....	—	—	—	—				
Norton Fitzwarren	M	L	....	—	—	M	L	M	L	M	L
Silkmill	—	—	....	—	—	—	—				
Fairwater Sidings	—	—	....	—	F						
Taunton West Stn.	R	L	....	G	L	M	L	R	L	R	L
TAUNTON	12 40	12 45	....	1224E	T1250	12 47		12 42	12 50	12 53	1 0
Taunton East Jct.	R	L	..	—	—	M	L	R	L	R	L
Creech Junction	R12	49L	..	R12	36L	M12	49L	R12	54L	R1	4L
Creech St. M. Halt	—	—	..	—	—	—	—	—	—	—	—
Cogload	—	—	..	—	—	—	—	—	—	R	L
Durston	—	—		—	—	—	—	—	—		
Lyng Halt	..	..								..	..
Athelney	....	....		..	..	—	—	..	..	....	....
Curry Rivel Jct.	....	....		..	..	—	—	..	..	....	....
Langport East	....	....		..	..	—	—	..	..	....	....
Long Sutton & P'ney	....	....		..	..	—	—	..	..	....	....
Somerton (Som.)	....	....		..	..	—	—	..	..	....	....
Charlton Mackrell	....	....		..	..	—	—	..	..	....	....
Keinton Mandeville	....	....		..	..	—	—	..	..	....	....
Alford Halt	..	..		..	..	—	—	..	..	....	....
Castle Cary ..←–■	..	..		..	..	—	—	..	..	....	....
Westbury	....	....		....	....	1 18		..	..	....	....
BRIDGWATER (Gen.)	1 0	1 3	....	—	—	—	—	1 7	1 11	1-16	1 20
Dunball	—	—		—	—	—	—	—	—	—	—
Pottery Siding	—	—		—	—	—	—	—	—	—	—
Highbridge (W.)←–■	1	12		1	27	—	—	1	21	1	29
Bristol	1 55	2 5		2 36C	T2 46	....	....	2 0	2 12	....	..
Paddington	..	..				3 30	—	..	..	..	..

Q—At Newton Abbot East Up Home Signal (Through Road) to detach B.E.

work these schedules are formed up. One notes such detail as the 'slip' coach attached to the Cornish Riviera Limited; detaching coaches without stopping is an artistic facet of operation that now, alas, is just history. (It will be enlarged upon later.)

The play that was put on using these documents as a script was fabulous, particularly as each week's show varied from the previous one, both in *ad lib.* ways as well as in those laid down in the Weekly Operating Notice. In this one notices such things as trains running in several parts in a timetable that was already too full of them singly. A vivid account of what happened is available to us in David St John Thomas's *Summer Saturdays in the West* (David & Charles, 1973).

None of these documents appears by magic. In railway back rooms all over the world many dedicated people work long hours to make this formidable multiple combination of jigsaw and crossword puzzle come out. The application of computers is on the point of making big changes in this area; not the least of their advantages is that it will no longer be necessary in Britain to finalize next year's timetable before any experience has been gained with this year's.

3 · ON SHED

Then .007 . . . asked what sort of a thing a hot-box
might be? 'Paint my bell sky-blue!' said Poney,
the switcher . . . 'Break me up and cast me into
five-cent sidewalk-fakirs' mechanical toys! . . .
You're too innocent to be left alone with your own
tender. Oh, you – you flat-car!"

RUDYARD KIPLING, '.007' (from *The Day's Work*)

Most of Kipling's famous short story '.007' (written long before
Ian Fleming or James Bond were born or thought of) took place
inside a North American locomotive shed in the 1880s. It concerns imaginary locomotive conversations between new boy
No. .007 and the old hands. It is typical of Kipling that, without
any experience in the locomotive world, he portrayed the ambience so exactly in this vivid, imaginative and eminently readable
little story. Only in one thing could his judgement be questioned:
he begins, 'A railway locomotive is, next to a marine engine, the
most sensitive thing man ever made.' In this respect no one who
has read as far as this could possibly admit that steam locomotives could yield top place to anything.

So, having looked up our train, we might, before going to catch
it, pay our homage at the place where it is being got ready. Every
vehicle from a jumbo jet to a bicycle needs preparation before
use. Railway trains are no exception. Well out of sight in sheds
and depots, railwaymen are engaged on the tedious tasks necessary before anyone's train can go. Although shed foremen no
longer feel behind the backs of the wheels of a locomotive with

white gloves to see whether it is ready to go out in traffic, and although shortcomings in cleanliness do not now lead to serious penalties for those responsible, this is far from being the case when it comes to safety. Any dereliction of duty here still leads even in these effete days to severe disciplinary action.

Because of the great responsibilities a locomotive driver bears, there is quite a tendency for him in time to become a kind of elder statesman, especially in smaller places. Aspiring locomotive engineers just out of their apprenticeship would be sent to take charge of such men. The immense respect with which they were treated seemed at first absurd to one then young man of your author's acquaintance – until he realized that it was then up to him to earn it.

You may think that locomotive sheds (or, for that matter, carriage sheds) have no art or romance about them, but it is not so. Artist David Shepherd found as much beauty there amongst the dirt and chaos of the dying age of steam as he did amongst elephants in the wild scenery of the African bush, as he recounts in his recent autobiography, *The Man Who Loves Giants* (David & Charles, 1975). As a man much more directly involved, Richard Hardy speaks in his autobiography (*Steam in the Blood*, Ian Allan, 1973) with great warmth of the time he spent and the people he met while in charge of various locomotive depots.

The true railway-lover has no such doubts about the attraction of the sheds where the objects of his affection live when they are at home. Should he happen to find himself in, say, Agra, India, he would certainly 'do the shed' first and visit the Taj Mahal second. Actually there are two sheds in Agra, both of them even today (1981) brim full of steam engines, although just recently environmental experts have adjudged the continued existence of both the 'Taj' and the steam sheds to be incompatible. Even so, that both should be there at all for fortunate visitors who appreciate them is as much to the credit of Anglo-American co-operation as to India, for not only do the still British-style railways there mostly have motive power of American design, but the Taj Mahal itself was saved from falling into ruin by the influence of the beautiful American wife of British Viceroy Lord Curzon.

Sheds with steam engines allocated to them are more interesting for all sorts of reasons. Steam locomotives need more servicing than diesels, so not only is there more going on but more of the fleet is at home being worked on. No one visiting a steam depot now can for a moment forget that such motive power is also a vanishing species; but even apart from that, steam is steam and has its own extra magic.

There are fairly good reasons for not allowing people to wander at will in yards and depots, mainly connected with the fact that rail vehicles cannot stop quickly or swerve to avoid a careless visitor. In consequence, shedmasters are prone to give the full 'Trespassers William' treatment to casual walkers-on. Challenged by one of them long ago, the author recalls giving a cheeky answer, 'We're ferro-equinologists, sir,' which did not however get the Order of the Boot it deserved. More recently, in far-off China, during an 'off-limits' search for steam, a very polite, gentle and charming man got off his bicycle and made an effort to communicate by searching for the appropriate character group in the phrase book. When he pointed to one against which the English meaning was given as 'prison', it seemed best to thank him politely, turn about and make off in the reverse direction as nonchalantly as possible.

Of course, whether in Soochow or Kentish Town, locomotive needs are exactly the same. Steam engines require large quantities of coal (usually) and water putting into them and quite large amounts of ash and other waste products taking out of them. They need careful and thorough oiling and inspection as well as a periodic overhaul of bearings and other parts which can become worn. Some break down and have to be set aside awaiting repair while others (often of old, interesting and non-standard types) are also put aside at the end of their useful lives, awaiting breaking-up. Yet others, full up and ready to go, await what the

Americans call the 'ready tracks' for the traffic department of the railway to have a use for them. Naturally, any party going round with official blessing (much the best way really) will see all this. What they will not have pointed out but may still see will be such things as the pair of ruts, 55 inches apart, that existed for so long in Station Road, Cambridge. A 'Claud Hamilton' 4–4–0, carelessly driven while 'on shed', had come through the hoardings that surrounded the depot area. One can also keep a look-out for locomotive-shaped patches of lighter brickwork in walls at the ends of shed tracks.

Outside Britain and British-influenced territories steam-age locomotive sheds usually take the form of so-called 'roundhouses'. A roundhouse covered a series of tracks or stalls radiating from a turntable, the turntable itself remaining in the open, as in the sketch. In truth, 'curved house' would be a better name

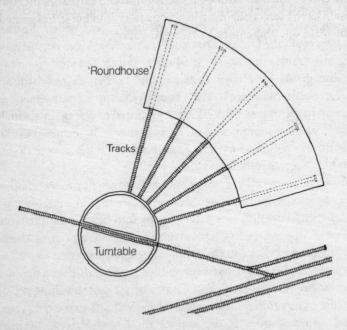

Curved house or roundhouse?

for the structure, but 'roundhouse' came to be the term normally used. In the U.S.A. 'roundhouse' has come to mean any locomotive depot, even now that oblong sheds ('squarehouses', perhaps) are the fashion under dieseldom. One objection to the roundhouse is that a little carelessness with the throttle and brake before the turntable is properly lined up means a locomotive going head-first into the turntable pit. Every locomotive in the shed is then immobilized!

Talking of unauthorized movements made by steam engines, Kipling's fantasy of imagining them as live beings is not so fanciful when one considers the times they have moved without human agency. A tiny leak in the throttle valve can cause steam pressure to build up in the cylinders, and suddenly the engine will move. In a roundhouse this is soon followed by contact with the end of the stall road or a plunge into the turntable pit, but there have been occasions when a runaway iron horse has gained the main line and enjoyed a riderless gallop.

4 · TERMINUS

The two-forty-five express – Paddington to
Market Blandings, first stop Oxford – stood at
the platform with that air of well-bred reserve
that is characteristic of Paddington trains.

P. G. WODEHOUSE,
Uncle Fred in the Springtime

There is both the *Good Food Guide* and the *Good Hotel Guide*,
not to speak of Penguin Books' own *Good Boat Guide* – each of
them nicely sent up by that small but succinct *Good Loo Guide*.
A *Good Terminus Guide* – from the railways enthusiasts' point of
view, of course – would be a worthwhile idea. Excluded completely would be stations from whose public areas and con-
courses the trains cannot be properly observed; such widespread
and otherwise stupendous edifices as New York's Grand Central
Terminal, Peking's Main Station or even our own Euston would
have to make do with five-star entries in some other book.

Additional marks would be awarded to termini for such things
as high overall roofs, stationmasters habitually in top hats, foot-
briges halfway down long platforms for observation, plus, of
course, a hefty marking for engineering or architectural
magnificence. A very special award might be reserved for termini
with steam, but if a terminus is defined as one with at least four
platform lines all ending in buffer stops, only one steam terminus
exists in the whole of Western Europe and North America –
Aberystwyth in mid-Wales. Belgrade would be another possible
but doubtful candidate; doubtful not only because Yugoslavia is

hardly 'in the West' but also because her railways have now hardly any steam. Incidentally, if Lawrence Durrell's enchanting story about Yugoslav trains called 'The Ghost Train' (from *Esprit de Corps*, Faber & Faber) is to be believed, some more of those highly significant ruts used to exist across the main concourse of Belgrade Station in those far-off steam days of thirty years ago. Wheel ruts across the concourse would certainly lift a mediocre station into the top class. In Washington, D.C., a giant electric locomotive once forgot it wasn't a person and came through the ticket barrier on to the concourse, which, being built for people, not locos, collapsed, letting the engine down into the basement. The incident was used as the climax of an excellent train movie called *Silver Streak*, starring Gene Wilder. The crash was superbly staged in an old aircraft hangar.

Even though for legal reasons it is not always possible for a real-life tourist guide to do so (except perhaps on the subject of rail travel), a good hypothetical one would award black marks or blots as well as marks for merit. One might begin with main stations in big cities which are not connected with that city's underground or rapid transit, such as Madrid's otherwise fabulous new Chamartín Station. Normally before taking a train journey one should have a nice preliminary rail 'fix' on an underground, a tube or a rapid-transit train. These all have very much their own ambience and attraction. Without doubt the Paris Métro is awarded the top prize: every main-line terminus is served and, moreover, the trains run the gamut from the very latest and most up-to-date down to (or perhaps up to) Edwardian relics still providing excellent service. On the way, the range of equipment in use takes in some fascinating rubber-tyred subway trains. The complicated system provides separate seats not only for first- and second-class travel but also for such classes of people as *femmes enceintes* and *les grands mutilés de la guerre*.

Talking of subways, some American friends of your author complained to him that they could never find their way down on to the London Underground. It transpired that they had several times gone down stairs marked 'Subway' but failed to find any trains at the bottom of them! But U.S.A. subways which do have trains in them and, like the Paris Métro, include some fine elevated railways are certainly worthy of the rail-fan's interest. Their complicated routes attracted the attention of science-fiction writer A. J. Deutsch, who wrote a short story entitled 'A Subway Named Mobius', based on the Boston system. It tells how a Harvard University Professor of Mathematics became concerned about the strange mathematical properties of the subway network, once the 'Boylston Shuttle had finally tied together the seven principal lines on four different levels'. When a Cambridge to Dorchester train suddenly disappeared one day, his suggestion to the authorities that the connectivity of the system had become infinite and accordingly the train was still on the system but without any real 'where' did not help. The story reappeared recently, suddenly without warning like its missing subway train, in an anthology called *100 Years of Science Fiction*, Book I (Pan Books, 1977).

Which brings us to one rather nice feature of all railway termini – the bookstalls, to which we might repair in order to stock up for Chapter 17 to come. But first there is the question of tickets. Here recent changes, like the disappearance of steam, have also not been for the better, since British Rail and other lines seem to be moving away from the traditional card railway ticket, known by its inventor's name as the Edmundson type. The horrible little bits of paper handed out instead are no substitute, particularly for those inflicted with that form of railway mania whose main symptom is the collection of railway tickets. The key attraction of this pastime is that it offends against at least one railway bye-law, for tickets are supposed to be collected from you, not by you. Soon enough (as with steam) only amateur-run railways will offer Edmundson tickets.

Serious Edmundson tickets covered a vast variety. There are the familiar singles and returns, but once there was third as well as first and second class. Excursions, tickets for some special train, platform tickets, provision for children, railwaymen, H.M. Forces and even dogs were other examples, the permutations amongst which led to infinite variety. More exotic items range from, say, admission tickets to an address by His Grace the Archbishop of York to the North-Eastern Railway Lecture & Debating Society to tickets incorporating little tabs which when pulled out might be found to be advertisements for patent medicines. No collector of railway tickets (and it is still a delightfully unspoilt and uncommercialized hobby) can ever complain of lack of material – even if he confined himself to ordinary single tickets and Britain alone, there were (without going back before 1935) say, 5,000 stations issuing them, with an average of perhaps thirty printed tickets to frequently used destinations. Combined with the other dimensions of variety, perhaps one million would be the ultimate count of a possible British Railway ticket collection.

As regards ticket selling, we award a specially large blot to those large stations whose multiple ticket windows have ill-labelled specialist functions, so that, having worked your way to the head of the queue, the clerk has the pleasure of saying 'two windows along for tickets to York' and you have to join another queue. But ticket clerks can be human, like the Anglo-Indian one at Bombay Victoria terminus who, when a homesick British serviceman half seriously asked for a 'third single to Leicester', answered (with a considerable amount of oneupmanship), 'Midland or London Road, sir?' Apocryphal or not, this well-known story makes the point that knowledgeable railway enthusiasts can crop up anywhere.

Less well received was a similar incident (in this case certainly true, for a colleague of your author was the culprit) given over the public address system at Utrecht Station, Holland, one morning in 1945. A coast-bound ambulance train formed of the very distinctive teak-built carriages of the London & North Eastern Railway rolled in and he could not resist announcing over the public address system that 'the train now standing at platform 1 is for Newcastle, calling at Grantham, Doncaster, York and Darlington ...' Every window in the train dropped, and the matron in charge of the train was not at all pleased. But aesthetically and from a rail-fan's point of view the incident was quite perfect.

So, with a brief reminder to award further blots to stations whose public address system announcements are loud but so bad acoustically that no one – even those who speak the language in which they are thought to be made – can make out the meaning, we go in search of our train. Again the French have a slight advantage here, but this time fortuitously, because of a quirk of language. In French 'grand' just means 'big', but in English the word has a connotation of magnificence, so a sign which says GRANDES LIGNES is much more thrilling than one which just says MAIN LINE PLATFORMS. Fortunately most of the world's termini supplement unintelligible public address with clear indicator boards giving the platform as well as station served for each departure. On the continent of Europe, regard has to be taken of the complex composition of trains, with up to six types of accommodation (first and second class in sleeper, couchette and ordinary carriage) going through to several different destinations. There are often cabinets of little cardboard model trains to help you find out the position of the carriage you want.

The art of choosing a good seat in the train is one which any regular traveller quickly achieves, but for the railway enthusiast it possesses other dimensions. Should he sit near the front to record the noise of the engine? At the back so that the train can be seen even on gentle curves, or so that after the engine reverses at X he will be at the front? In some interesting coach? On the best side to see the mile posts? And so on.

So far it has been assumed that we intend to avail outselves of what is one of the great yet completely unappreciated advantages of rail travel – the freedom just to step on and go. Even though tickets have been bought, the railway company or ticket agent was not told our names or by which train we were travelling; indeed, the ticket usually implies we have the choice of any train over a number of days (unless we are to occupy reserved seats or berths, which on many top trains are obligatory).

One thing that the careful traveller, whether booked or unbooked, rail-fan or just plain human, should now do is to see if a refreshment car is, first, there at all and, second, if there, whether it looks like being activated. Then, if the omens are unfavourable, there is time to buy a picnic from the buffet which, one might add, usually nowadays offers better food and drink than the ancient awful reputation of railway fare might indicate. This is not to say, of course, that people (not in Britain anyway) find railway terminus food worth a detour when they are not travelling, even if they are keen railway enthusiasts.

On the other hand, as railway enthusiasts, it is well on the cards that they might have come to the station not to catch a train but just to enjoy the play – in fact, to see something of what the artist Frith saw when he made his famous picture *The Railway Station*. His model was Paddington Station, London, easily recognizable even now, some 130 years later. The faces of the crowd are all well-known figures of the day, the degree of dignity in their portrayal being in inverse proportion to the pomposity of their public image. Talking of Paddington, the late Professor Tuplin wrote in *Great Western Saints and Sinners* (George Allen & Unwin, 1971): 'Being in the neighbourhood with some time to spare, Mr Harrison had gone into Paddington Station to see the down (Cornish Riviera) Limited go out at 10.30 am and perhaps also the departure of the 10.45. Many people . . . have then found themselves watching the 3.30 pm go before being forced to come to the conclusion that it really was time they went themselves!' Your present author is certainly one of the people referred to, but the 'Harrison' of this story (which one suspects is largely autobiographical) realized that the unthinkable had happened because the inpeccable 'Limited' was delayed and set off behind

a lesser locomotive. Thinking that there might be some fire-
works, he jumped on board and recorded an unforgettable
journey. But train-timing and locomotive matters come elsewhere in this book, the latter in the next chapter.

5 · MOTIVE POWER

'. . . The man that drives the engine. Why, his
smoke alone is worth a thousand pounds a puff.'

LEWIS CARROLL,
Alice Through the Looking Glass

In this Delectable Country of Enthusiasm for Railways which we
are exploring, no area is more delectable or attracts more of the
fraternity than the motive power itself. It has taken a knock
recently as diesel and electric traction has gradually taken over
from steam. Certainly, it does not help that, even when the new
motive power is not an integral part of the train, it looks very like
an ordinary bogie carriage or van. With steam one can look inside
the cab at the great furnace which is the source of all the power
and admire the rods which transmit that power to the wheels.
Furthermore, for historical rather than engineering reasons, the
number of types (that is, wheel arrangements) of steam on any
railway were likely to be ten or fifteen times as many as with diesel
or electric. So variety was lost as well as the thrill.

From all accounts people were just as sad when the iron
(steam) horse was substituted for the flesh-and-blood kind, but
here it was a case of *force majeure* – costs and timings were slashed
by a factor of some four or five times. In our case (and without
uselessly crying over spilt milk for more than a moment),
modern steam power maintained with first-rate facilities was
hardly ever compared on equal terms with modern diesel power.
Even when on rare occasions the terms of comparison between
steam and diesel were reasonably equal, the case for substitution

was not a very good one. In Britain, expensive coal from ancient coal mines with small seams combined with easy access to oil fuel did, however, make a fair case for dieselization. One might ask whether steam could make a comeback here when the oil runs out. The answer of course is 'yes', but it would be more likely to reappear in the form of a few more steam-driven turbo-generators in electric power stations, which would provide the power for electric trains, than in the form of new steam engines. The unlikely possibility of a small 'real' steam operation in Britain early next century is discussed in the final chapter of *How to Drive a Steam Locomotive* (Penguin Books, 1981). Perhaps, though, one could be just a little more sanguine about steam in South Africa, Zimbabwe, India or China lasting into the foreseeable future. More to the point, as this book is being written it is announced that a firm called American Coal Enterprises Inc. has designed an up-to-date 4–8–2 steam locomotive and is raising 25 million dollars to produce two prototypes.

It is difficult to imagine any steam locomotive which could emulate what is possible with electric traction. Just as the hay-burning horse can never hope to emulate what the coal-burning steam loco can do, so that in its turn has to yield price of place to the electric tractor, with all the surging output of big power stations available to it. But it should never be said that steam would have been unable to attain the speeds and power outputs of diesel prime-movers today. The power cars of Britain's magnificent H.S.T. 125 (125-mph high-speed trains) develop some 4,500 horse-power. Powers of this magnitude were developed in the cylinders of some modern steam locomotives, although to get such power combined with big wheels for high speeds inside the British loading gauge, it would be necessary to go in for the double Beyer-Garratt type. With some of the latest electric trains, the installed horse-power reaches 12,000; faced with such an output, of course, even the most dyed-in-the-wool steam fan must acknowledge that his favourite steeds must yield pride of place.

For the railway enthusiast, the saddest thing about the change has still been that suppression of variety. Worldwide the picture is worse. In steam days most nations had distinctive steam locomotives and many countries, even small and agricultural ones, built their own. Ireland, Norway, Finland, New Zealand, Holland, Switzerland, Denmark and Romania were very surprising candidates for self-reliance in locomotive production. The same applied to individual railways in larger countries, the prize being without doubt awarded to Wales's own Festiniog Railway, whose little Boston Lodge Works have built three for their thirteen-mile line during the last one-and-a-half centuries (in 1879, 1885 and 1979!). Alas, most other loco builders now do so no more, for the economical production of diesel-electric locomotives means concentration of manufacture and mass-production methods. It also means that, with only minor modifications and different-colour paint, the same locomotives can be seen in Wichita, Valparaiso and Kimberley. Of course, variety is not a necessary concomitant of steam; perhaps its continued survival – and continued construction – in China may be partly due to there being effectively only six types of steam locomotive running in that vast country.

Countries in which there is even today a chance that one might find a steam locomotive at the head end of one's train are Angola, Bangladesh, China, East Germany, Indonesia, India, Mozambique, Pakistan, Poland, South Africa, Turkey, Vietnam and Zimbabwe. Other countries in which one might see a working steam locomotive out of the windows are Austria, Greece, Italy, Jordan, Sudan and Zambia, as well as most South American countries. Of course, this does not include steam locomotives run for pleasure. Britain, for example, could field a steam-for-fun fleet greater than a number of the countries listed above have of steam-for-business trains.

The effect of the passing of workaday steam upon railway enthusiasts has been to spread their interests. Those who just had to go on getting their steam 'fixes' began to go further and further afield. Some started to take more of an interest in the railways as a whole and others went into preservation or even modelling. These defections have been compensated for by the expansion of the hobby and this has meant that perhaps nearly as many 'boys of all ages' do a bit of train-watching at Paddington as did before. But no one setting off to the west by Cornish Riviera Limited nowadays makes the traditional pigrimage up to the front to see the engine – this for one very good reason: it hasn't got one.

Even so, locomotives are the prime interest of the railway enthusiast and perhaps the following advertisement which appeared in the *Railway Magazine* for March 1981 shows the lengths to which this interest is carried:

> Can anyone tell me the numbers of the locos which worked the 10.40 Exmouth to Cleethorpes train between Temple-combe and Bath (Green Park) on Sat. 6th August, 1960? – Reply etc. . . . .

It is fairly impressive that there should have been an Exmouth to Cleethorpes train at all in the timetable, let alone that someone should have recorded and kept the numbers of its locomotives on a particular day over twenty years ago. But that anyone should pay good money to find out those numbers after all this length of time might seem a trifle strange to anyone not interested in ferro-equinology – and even a few of the converted might raise an eyebrow.

Recording numbers, and in de-luxe cases names, carries a young man (for some reason it is not a thing girls do) in due time on to an appreciation of the finer points of design; in the days of steam one could even make out a good deal for oneself. In any case most youngsters have, like Kipling's young friend, 'seven million whys' in their vocabulary, while with older railway enthusiasts the problem is not starting them talking about locomotives, but stopping them. This is a combination that produces results.

Locomotives, especially steam ones, have their own beauty.

The faithful talk of a Stanier, a Gresley, a Baldwin, a Church-ward or a Chapelon in the same way that art lovers might talk of a Botticelli, a Gauguin, a Modigliani or a Constable. Paintings are of course at a disadvantage compared with locomotives, which are not only three-dimensional but also have movement, as well as producing their own kind of music. So sculpture, ballet and concert music also enter into any parallels that the fanciful might draw.

This book has so far been uniformly unkind towards steam's successors. But this aesthetic inferiority was not always the case, and one man in particular is noted specially for an artistic approach to using the infernal combustion engine for transport. He was a genius amongst artist-engineers and his name was Count Ettore Bugatti. David Curwen, that veteran builder of small steam locomotives, was once telling several of us that if you approached Bugatti with a view to buying one of his cars he would ask you to lunch to check that you were a fit person to have one. In fact, it was just like having a locomotive from David Curwen, as one of his audience remarked.

It is less generally known that Bugatti did great things on *rails* with a series of remarkable railcars and trains, mainly in France. They were low-built and driven from a conning tower in the centre. Panoramic views were thus available for passengers seated at both ends, and smooth riding was achieved by the use of eight-wheel bogies instead of the more usual four. Power was provided by either two or four of the famous Bugatti 200-hp 'Royale' engines. During October 1934 an 800-hp 'Presidential' type car achieved a speed (then a record for France) of 120 mph on test. Bugatti also worked on a high-speed steam train for the French railways. Unusual and imaginative features included the use of fast-revolving engine parts with small cylinders in multiple, and tenders with baggage and buffet compartments. When war came in 1939 work was stopped on the project – as on so many other similar ones elsewhere.

The proposition that the reduced attraction of diesel and

electric power compared with steam has its origin in the fact that
so little of the mechanism of the former is visible to our admiring
gaze gains support from the admiration lavished on vintage
electric locomotives. With most electric locomotives one can at
least observe the method of collecting current, with the delightful sparkings and concertina-ings of the pantograph. Even some
of the switch gear stands naked and unashamed on the roof. With
older machines, such as the 'Crocodile' electric locomotives of
the Swiss and Austrian Federal Railways, or the 'Baby
Crocodiles' of the narrow-gauge Rhaetian Railways, it is also
possible to see the way power is transmitted to the wheels. But,
also, even these delights are disappearing, replaced by modern
power with internal driving systems. How little consideration
modern traction engineers give to those who regard railways as
an art-form!

6 · GREEN FLAG

If there was one memory of that night which remained with the boys, it was the wondrous beauty of the signal lamps they passed.

H. R. MILLAR, *The Dreamland Express*

The starting of a great train is a moment to savour: the blowing of whistles, the shouts (according to nationality) of ''Board', '*Attention au départ*', '*Einsteigen*' or 'Right away', and finally the waving of a green flag or lamp before the train moves off. This is perhaps the moment to say that with very few exceptions every move made on a railway is ordered by systems of signals. To many people (and certainly to your author) the art of signalling is one of the most fascinating of all aspects of railways. The very fact that it was born and evolved in death and destruction only serves to increase one's strength of feeling towards something which must be precious if only because the price paid has been so high.

Trains on the world's railways can be signalled in any of three basic ways. The first is by the timetable; that is to say, the time-table is written so that trains shall not collide. Naturally there has to be a procedure, usually by issuing what are called train orders, for trains running extra, running out of course or cancelled; this system had (and to some extent has) its finest flowering in North America, but subsidiary lines in continental Europe and elsewhere have similar arrangements. There need not be any fixed signals under this system, but there are some rather delightful special ones like the all-weather fuzees which can be put down on the track behind a train which is, perhaps, getting behind schedule. They burn for a fixed time, say five minutes, and if the driver of a following train sees the light of a fuzee at night or its smoke by day, he knows he must run rather cannily from then on. Another kind of firework used to supplement all systems of signalling is the torpedo (in English English, detonator) which can be fixed to the rail in ones, twos or threes. They make big bangs as wheels pass over.

More familiar to British readers is the 'block' system whereby the signalman at A only lowers the signals for a train to go to B once he has ascertained from the signalman at B that the line is clear, that is, that the previous train has passed intact. Under this system the signals normally show stop, unless there is a train coming and all is clear.

Replacing both these kinds of signalling on lines of any importance is automatic signalling, whereby the signals normally show clear whether there is a train coming or not. As a train goes past a signal, its presence on the track is detected and the signal changes to 'Stop'. Later, a 'Caution' indication is given (sometimes two successively less cautious 'Cautions' are provided) and, finally, when the train ahead is detected as being the full braking distance ahead, the signal shows 'Clear' again.

Almost quite obsolete, although still provided for in the British Rule Book to be used in cases where communications have broken down, is the time-interval system of working. In the railways' early days the danger signal was exhibited by a railway policeman for, say, three minutes after a train had gone by and the caution signal for between three and ten minutes afterwards.

Some freight-only railways and lines in Britain are still operated in the same way as the Stockton & Darlington Railway was operated, that is, the drivers must just look out for and keep clear of trains in front just as one does when driving one's car on a road. With brakes provided only on the locomotive (no brake vans were used), the operation could be fairly described as a somewhat hairy procedure.

Each of these systems has its own way of dealing with trains on single lines. The timetable or train order system becomes just that bit trickier to operate if what are sometimes called 'cornfield meets' are to be avoided. Traditionally the man in charge (the despatcher) got out by the back window and vanished for ever when he realized that he had made a mistake resulting in one. In North America, the composing of train orders within the standard operating rules, prescribed to give maximum efficiency in operation together with economy in words used, is a high art. An elementary guide to the preliminaries is included in *How to Drive a Steam Locomotive*.

Talking of books, in each chapter of this one so far, mention has been made of the relevant literature. With signalling, though, there is a problem because it is one of the few big holes in the whole vast field of railway books. The standard textbook on the subject, *Railway Signalling and Communications* (published by the trade journal *Railway Gazette*), is not only rather solid fare but also out of print. However, Adrian Vaughan's superb *A Pictorial History of Great Western Signalling* (Oxford Publishing, 1973) waxes lyrical on every page about the poetry that was G.W.R. signalling, and is also reasonably comprehensive in respect of the basic principles of the art.

On single lines in Britain, and elsewhere in places where British influence has been important, the block system is reinforced by arrangements for giving the driver a physical token of authority to proceed. It could be a staff, a key, a tablet or even a ball, clearly marked with the places between which it applies. In the elementary form of this system there is only one of these tokens, so that if a driver has it with him he can enter a single-line section secure in the knowledge that no one else is going to. Since this arrangement has limitations – for example, what happens if there are two consecutive trains needing to go in the same direction? – the electric single-line token system was evolved in which a number of tokens are held in a matched and connected pair of instruments, one at either end of the section. Their hefty brassy Victorian mechanisms are arranged so that only one token can be removed at one time, but from either end. Once it has been removed the remaining tokens are locked in the instrument until the one removed has been put back. Again the token can be a staff, a key, a ball or a tablet. Tablets can crop up in surprising places: once, during a journey on a Japanese engine at a place where a double line changed to single, a single-line token was handed up; the interpreter turned to your author and said, 'In Japanese we call that a *tab-let*'.

If North America (and particularly western North America) is the spiritual home of the train order, the Highlands of Scotland are the place to go for token signalling. In addition to the pouch-and-hoop arrangement used for exchanging tokens by hand, there still exists on some Highland lines and in a few other places a system for exchanging tokens automatically as a train runs through a station at which it does not stop. It can be done at speeds up to 60 mph, and it is fascinating to watch as the arm on the engine is swung out to engage with the arm on the lineside apparatus. Automatic token exchange is the last to exist of four highly thrilling on-the-run railway operations; the others – the picking-up of water, the dropping and picking-up of mail bags, and the slipping of carriages – are no longer to be seen anywhere in the world.

Your author had a wonderful introduction to the world of single-line signals during the Second World War when school summer holidays were occupied with harvest camps. Naturally the one with the greatest distance by rail from his home in the south seemed the most attractive proposition, and the absence of such superfluities as a seat to sit down on during the long journey to Scotland was unnoticed in the thrill of going north of Potters Bar for the first time.

The camp was near Fearn Station, forty-one miles north of Inverness, 609 from Euston and still, amazingly, open. What had been a leisurely existence for the little station ceased abruptly with the declaration of war and became a continuous block-and-block operation with double-headers all through the day and night, including the famous 'Jellicoe Express' through from Euston to Thurso, mainly for the Royal Navy. But none of this prevented the hard-pressed staff from showing off the delights of their station's surprisingly complex signalling to two or three interested youngsters. The station with short platform was at the north end of a loop long enough to take a double-headed fifteen-coach train, while the signal box was at the south end, nearly a quarter of a mile away. The tablet instruments were in the office, the facing points at the station end were worked from a tin shelter on the platform, while the tablet exchange apparatus was even further from the signal box, north of the loop. For the porter-signalman on duty, working a train past the station meant two visits to each of these locations, and we were able to repay the kindness shown a little by taking a few of the more foolproof of these chores off his hands in the evenings. But even now the thrill of standing by the tablet-catcher as the Up 'Further North Mail' came through in the dark behind two of the legendary 'Black Five' 4-6-os remains vividly in the memory.

A quite delightful development of the signalling on this 'Further North' line has come in the last few years. A blizzard – during which trains were stranded for days in romantic Murder-on-the-Orient-Express style – brought down most of the telegraph wires and many poles. It was both quicker and cheaper to restore communications by means of microwave radio links than by restoring the pole routes. In order to achieve an integrity of communication sufficient to allow the connections between the token instruments to be by radio, the plain direct-current impulses produced by these vintage Victorian devices were converted by a micro-processor to a special code, which was sent over the air three times to the similar micro-processor at the other end of the section. This little computer then compared the signals it received, decided that they were genuine, converted

Elizabethan electricity back to Victorian and the instrument at the other station responded as if the two of them had been connected by wires.

North American railways make much more use of radio than others, most of it in railway talk between drivers, brakemen, guards, tower-men and despatchers. This has opened up a whole new area of railway pleasure, as of course radio communication, unlike telephone communication, is also radio broadcasting. *Trains Magazine* is full of advertisements for 'scanner' radio sets which are specially suitable for receiving the frequencies which railroads use. By their means one can eavesdrop in a really intimate way on the no doubt frequently riveting conversations between railroadmen at work. Conceptually, of course, it might be possible through radio to interfere with railway operations, although a very intimate knowledge of both the principles and the details involved would be needed to do so successfully.

The most glaring case of interference with signalling was that mail train robbery to end them all which took place some twenty years ago in England between Rugby and Euston. Early one morning, not just one but two automatic colour-light signals situated three-quarters of a mile apart were masked and replaced with battery lanterns, between the passing of one train and the next. The driver found nothing out of the ordinary in the aspects of the spurious signals and stopped as the robbers intended.

Crimes with signalling are not quite common enough affairs to be the subject of a book, but cases do occur, most much less serious and some even amusing. For example, one precaution against malpractice in most signal boxes is the signal-box register, a large record book in which the signalman writes down what he does and to the minute when he does it. This book has to be available for inspection at all times, but imagine the surprise of a Signalling Inspector, visiting a box which controlled a level crossing at the entrance to a certain group of railway-owned docks, to find a spare signal-box register book that contained pictures and descriptions of nice ladies. It turned out that this signal box had a secondary role as a dating service for mariners coming ashore from newly arrived ships; further investigation indicated that the signalmen took their commission (it was rationing time) in such things as ship's butter, meat and cheese.

We have now ranged rather widely over the whole field of the little-known art of railway signalling. It is the author's hope that sufficient has been said to inspire some readers to make the effort to learn more about one of the fascinating aspects of the world's railway systems.

7 · ROLLING ALONG

Faster than fairies, faster than witches,
Bridges and houses, hedges and ditches;
And charging along like troops in a battle,
All through the meadows with horses and cattle:
All of the sights of the hill and the plain
Fly as thick as the driving rain;
And even again, in the wink of an eye,
Painted stations whistle by.

ROBERT LOUIS STEVENSON,
From a Railway Carriage

Stevenson's enjoyment of travelling by train was such that he broke into immortal verse, and this is how so many rail-lovers feel when rolling along even some entirely familiar railway. This feeling hardly changes whether one is looking out on to Scenery with a capital S or seeing the back gardens of a sprawling city's suburbs. The world is somehow quite unselfconscious about being looked at from a railway, whereas towards a road all is lace curtains and respectability. It would be nice to experiment and see whether the lace curtain treatment continued if the train ran down the road, but such places as Syracuse, New York, where the New York to Chicago main line of the New York Central Railroad once ran right along the main street, are now exceedingly rare.

Without any doubt, the top pleasure of a journey by train is the enjoyment of the passing scene. One suspects there is a romantic story to be written about someone who, from the train, gets to know the poeple who live in, say, a lineside farmhouse seen on a habitual journey. And how one day he can no longer bear not having met them and accordingly makes an excuse to call, naturally finding the daughter of the house as nice as she looked when seen from the train . . .

Of course one can make conversation in a train. This is easier for an Englishman if one of the party is foreign or, best of all, Welsh. During your author's habitual journey over the years from London to North Wales on the evening trains, people have tried such things as to make him believe in Spiritualism, recruit him (apparently) as a Communist agent and, once, just before leaving Euston, succeed in lifting £2.50 each from him and a friend with a tear-jerking and brilliantly told story of wife and child held at the ticket barrier because of lack of that sum. One pleasure yet to be savoured is the legendary card game (chemin-de-fer, of course) with strangers, against which all parents warn their sons.

Far removed from these journeys in the sealed air-conditioned 100-mph trains of the west-coast main line is one across the Rockies. Would you believe that among the possible things to do on a train is the sport of flying kites? The whole affair now seems like a dream, but with a train whose maximum speed was 25 mph, which had an open observation car at the rear (air-conditioned with real Colorado air) and on a railway where bridges and over-head cables were non-existent, kite-flying was not only possible but a pinnacle of enjoyment. It also happened that the writer's hat blew off while he was talking to the conductor. The latter immediately stopped the train and we walked back to collect it. Such was personal service on the Denver & Rio Grande Western Railroad at a 10,000-foot altitude in 1964. In a normal railway train, one's view of the world outside is limited to a sideways one, but enclosed observation cars of both the 'dome' and the 'rear-end' types are still fairly common on this and other kindred railroads in North America, which carry the best trains through the best scenery. In Britain, by contrast, observation cars appear only on the humblest trains and only fortuitously amongst good scenery. The sort of elderly trains that thread the oil refineries, steel mills and chemical plants between, say, Darlington, Middlesbrough and Redcar have passenger windows at both ends and a superb view in this industrial Grand Canyon of railway signalling and furniture generally.

In contrast, not far away, the North Yorkshire Moors preserved railway has acquired one or two of these despised diesel multiple-unit trains, painted them in nice colours, packaged them as the National Park Scenic Cruise Train and finds visitors queueing up to travel at double the normal rate per mile. In fact, the same technique as Mark Twain's Tom Sawyer used when he had to paint the fence before going off to play and did it with such an air that his friends paid him to have a turn with the brush.

So much for the ways in which human beings might amuse themselves while rolling along – but what does a rail-fan do? The number one O.K. activity is to time the train. The greatest names in railway journalism, Charles Rous-Marten, Cecil J. Allen and O. S. Nock, have given priority to setting down, month by month over the last seventy-five years or so in the *Railway Magazine*, detailed logs of train running in Britain. 'British Locomotive Practice and Performance' the articles were called; now, very much a sign of the times, the word 'British' has been dropped. C.J.A. and O.S.N. went on to do the same thing in book after book.

How then do you time a train? The first requirement is to be even more English than the average English rail passenger as regards conversation with your travel companions. The next is to be specially ruthless in securing a corner seat facing the direction of travel and on the side where the mile-posts are located. You also need a list of timing points, including stations, tops of gradients and functions. A stop-watch or two and the traditional pencil sharpened at both ends completes the outfit. In addition to writing down times to the nearest second, one should take timings of the speed from the mile-posts and

Train: 7.20 pm Euston to Inverness 'The Royal Highlander'
(first of three parts), 11.8.39

Engine nos: 4767, 5428
Type: Class 5, 4–6–0
Drivers: B. A. McCleod, J. Urquhart
Load, empty: 450 (15 coaches)
Load, full: 480

Miles	Timing points	Schedule	mins.	secs.	Comments
0·0	Perth	0	0	00	
1·6	Almond Valley Junc.	—	3	25	
4·2	Luncarty	—	6	32	
7·2	Stanley	12	10	40	
10·3	Murthly	18	15	25	
12·9	Kingswood Crossing	22	18	50	
15·6	Dunkeld	25	21	53	
20·4	Dalguise	31	27	42	
23·6	Ballinluig	35	31	13	
28.5	PITLOCHRY	41	37	02	
29·7	Milepost 29¾	—	39	37	Top of grade
32·2	Killiecrankie	46	42	10	
35·3	BLAIR ATHOLL	52	46	35	
4·5	Struan	9	7	4	
9·3	Dalanraoch	—	16	25	
15·7	Dalnaspidal	34	29	26	
17·5	Druimachdar Summit	—	32	09	37 mph min.
23·3	Dalwhinnie	43	39	02	
33·4	Newtonmore	55	50	20	69 mph max.
36·3	KINGUSSIE	59	55	32	

quarter-mile-posts at critical places. The final touch is to ask the engine crew for their names, as well of course as ascertaining the weight and composition of the train. The approximate number of passengers is also a factor in that a full train may be some thirty tons heavier than an empty one. The second line of the old carriage designer's jingle 'sixteen to the bum, sixteen to the ton' is helpful here, the average passenger being considered to be sixteen inches wide and ten stone in weight, complete with clothes and belongings.

If there is no chance of a corner seat, speeds could be taken (in the days before welded rails) by counting the number of rail joints in forty-one seconds. This gives the speed in miles per hour assuming that the rails were sixty feet long, which was normally the case from, say, the 1930s until continuous welded rail became standard. The table shows what a good deal of concentrated observation could produce.

If you thought that there was anything remarkable about the run you could have sent it in with a commentary to Allen or Nock; in due time, maybe, you'd have then had the pleasure of seeing it in print with a kind word of thanks added. If speed limits had even slightly been exceeded, it was customary not to 'tell tales' and so the date and drivers' names would be omitted from the account.

Some (including this writer) may have thought that perhaps much of the detail set out in this stereotyped manner with some bland commentary was occasionally just a little overdone. However, the offerings were very well received by readers, including (and this is very impressive) the enginemen themselves. Even today, now that the variable performance of the steam locomotive – wayward mainly because of the variable performance of the human who fed it with coal – is replaced by more precise haulage with diesel or electric power, people still pass the journey occupied with this rather strange activity. The mantle of high priest of the cult has just now fallen on Peter Semmens of the National Railway Museum; the fact of his having more of a scientific and less of an engineering background than his predecessors may result in a new approach.

Having written a little bit of railway fiction himself, this writer it must be admitted does occasionally wonder how often irreverent jokers did a 'Piltdown Man' on the *Railway Magazine* logs of runs (like the example above), which are very easy to synthesize, although in this case one or two clues have been left in (loco 4767 was not built until 1946; neither 4767 nor 5428 was ever stationed in Scotland).

Talking of train-timing and jokes, *Punch* for 10 August 1949, 'with affectionate acknowledgements to Mr Cecil J. Allen of the *Railway Magazine*', carried an enchanting piece called 'British Motor-bus Practice and Performance' in a delightful parody of C.J.A.'s style, including a log and account of a run from Notting Hill Gate to Victoria. No one could ask for greater recognition than that.

Richard Wright, in his monumental tome on the Southern Pacific's high-speed 'Daylight' trains between Los Angeles and San Francisco (the size of a volume of *Encyclopaedia Britannica* for just one train), speaks of the 'bing-bong men' recording passing times at all the mile-posts on the 400-mile journey, in order to set the train's schedule. So train-timing is a professional activity even if it is not everybody's idea of the way to enjoy a railway journey.

One regrets that there is an element amongst the rail-fan Establishment that considers any passenger who just looks out and contents himself with enjoying the passing railway scene as being 'well, you know, not really quite our sort'. May one say that those who follow the party line in this respect miss a great deal? A railway's lineside furniture speaks volumes both for the kind of railway you are travelling on and for the traditions that brought it into being. You suddenly spot a pure English signal in India or the Argentine, or perhaps see an unmistakable Wagons-Lits sleeping-car body in use as a mess van outside Hong Kong, reminding those with eyes to see of a (never

fulfilled) proposal to run a sort of Far East Blue Train from
Hong Kong to Peking. Even the shape of the mile- and gradient-
posts is significant. Some railways even mark the radii of curves:
the narrow-gauge railways in the old princely state of Baroda
mark each curve with quite a little lecture on how it is set out:

Curve no.	12A
Length	105 m.
Radius	120 m.
Cant	45 mm.
Transition length	60 m.

Perhaps the old Gaekwar had a rather schoolmasterish taste in
engineers! He certainly had a feel for railways, and built a really
superb $10\frac{1}{4}$-inch gauge steam pleasure railway in the palace
grounds. The principal locomotive is, amazingly, a replica of an
ex-L.N.E.R. *Flying Scotsman* type 4–6–2. Now that Baroda is a
democratic Indian state, the line has become, without having to
move or, indeed, suffer much change, a public pleasure railway
in the Municipal Park. Incidentally, His Royal Highness of
Gwalior had a solid-silver model train specially made for him by
the once legendary English firm of Bassett-Lowke. The train
operated a refreshment service around his great banqueting-
room table. It travelled quite slowly, by all accounts, and when
a guest lifted the lid of one of the dish-cars it stopped automatically so that they could help themselves.

An apology is due, perhaps, for including here an item which
properly belongs in the chapter dealing with freight movement;
but it should refresh us before we come to the drawback to travelling by train which is that, if you travel in one, you can't watch
it or take photographs of it. A good compromise is to watch one
train and travel in another, while bringing your car with you; this
has been possible (with different types of vehicle) from Day One
of inter-city travel in 1830, but only recently has it become a
highly developed facility under the name (in Britain) of Motorail.
Some American friends of the writer's from Detroit toured

Britain this way, taking their car with them. The car – a small Vauxhall Viva – was provided gratis by their employers, General Motors. On returning, they told the agent they'd had it over the hundred more than once; horrified, he threatened to report them to the G.M. Society for the Prevention of Cruelty to Motor Cars, until they confessed the car's wheels hadn't been turning at the time.

On the other hand, *quite* the best way of both travelling and seeing a train is to go on one that offers run-pasts. That is, the train stops at a suitable scenic spot, everyone gets down on to the track and the train then backs away out of sight. Next, the loco-motive is opened up, the fireman turning up the oil-feed or shovelling in extra coal to make plenty of smoke, and the run-past takes place. Lastly, the train backs up once more to collect the passengers by the lineside. Most railway administrations would be frightened to death at the mere thought, but American railroad companies are made of sterner stuff and this operation occurs regularly when special trains are run over there for rail-fans, even on double-track main lines.

You may be surprised to learn that a run-past has even been made by request on an ordinary timetable train – this was in narrow-gauge India, on the Nadiad to Petlad line not far from Baroda. While the intention was unfaultable, the execution suffered a little from the fact that many of the passengers (who included not only standees but also clingers-on) ran past with the train!

Talking of instant changes to the timetable arrangements, one also remembers another occasion in that same accommodating country. The party was travelling from the hill resort of Matheran back to Bombay. Someone expressed disappointment to the stationmaster that a diesel locomotive was at the head of the train. 'You want steam, I put steam on,' he said. And he did.

8 · SPECIALS

'Already, you see,' said [Holmes]. Far away from
among the Kentish woods there arose a thin spray of
smoke. A minute later a carriage and engine could be
seen flying along the open curve which leads to the
station. We had hardly time to take our places behind
a pile of luggage when it passed with a rattle and a
roar.

A. CONAN DOYLE, 'The Final Problem'
(from *The Memoirs of Sherlock Holmes*)

If the pleasures of rolling along in an ordinary train are thought
of as x, then those of going by special train are as x squared. All
of us remember what happened in 'The Final Problem' when
Sherlock Holmes and Dr Watson gave Professor Moriarty the
slip by catching the Dover Boat Train at Victoria. One almost
feels sorry for the evil professor, who would have been too dis-
tracted by the urgent need to dispose of the great detective to
have really enjoyed chartering (and getting) a special at an
instant's notice. I wonder what the stationmaster there would say
today if anyone tried to do this.

Fiction aside, one man who did once manage it was soldier,
journalist, traveller and railway enthusiast Peter Fleming. It was
one evening in April 1940, when he had been sent back from
Norway with an urgent situation report to be delivered personally to the C.I.G.S. in Whitehall. Bad weather prevented flying
further than Inverness and Fleming found himself stranded
there; it was late on Saturday, the evening train to London had
gone and there was not another for twenty-four hours. He tenta-

tively approached the stationmaster who, as a proper railway-man, just said, 'When would you like to start, sir?' And so it was, even a sleeping car being provided; no doubt he felt like royalty. He described it all on B.B.C. Radio after the war.

Fleming had an urgent military reason, but others have done it just for fun. In July 1905, a miner, whose name was Walter Scott but who was known to history as Death Valley Scotty because he had struck it rich in the Nevada desert, felt that a reasonable first indulgence with his new-found wealth (one with which no true rail-fan would disagree) was a record-breaking special train run regardless of cost from Los Angeles to Chicago over the Atchison Topeka & Santa Fe Company's main line. With three cars they did the 2,246 miles in 44 hours 54 minutes instead of the then scheduled 63 hours. When one considers that both the Cajon and Raton passes had to be crossed and that the locomotives of the day needed watering every fifty miles or so and changing every hundred, the average speed of 50 mph is fairly remarkable. A 100-mph maximum speed was, it is said, attained on the stretch between Fort Madison and Galesburg, and legend also claims that Scotty himself gave some professional help with the firing.

In 1906 Kipling wrote up a similar journey in his novel *Captains Courageous*. It was made by a railway magnate called Harvey Cheyne, from San Diego to Chicago over the same Santa Fe route. He writes: 'Three bold and experienced men . . . swung her over the great lift from Albaquerque to Glorietta and beyond Springer, up and up to the Raton Tunnel on the state line, whence they dropped rocking into La Junta, had sight of the Arkansas [River], and tore down the long slope to Dodge City where Cheyne took comfort once again from setting his watch an hour ahead . . .

Railways have been under royal patronage ever since the young Queen Victoria, after consulting her dear Albert, decided to travel by train from Windsor to London on 13 June 1842. Brunel rode on the engine and Gooch drove the train personally.

Over the years since then royal journeys have become more of a routine for the railway authorities and a few of the special precautions originally taken have been relaxed. For example, it used to be that a pilot engine was sent in front of the Royal Train; I think in the end, after a near miss, it must have dawned on those concerned that there was likely to be more danger, not less, with a pilot engine always a block or two in front. Of course, no official likes to be the actual one who relaxes some precaution. Even as recently as fifteen years ago one found in the Royal Train instructions such phrases as: 'At level crossings where a gate-woman is in charge, a competent man shall be present half-an-hour before the Royal Train is due.' Bridges were guarded, stand-by engines provided, freight trains on adjacent lines halted and so on ... Very few untoward incidents have been known, not so much because of any special competence, but merely because a great deal of trouble was taken. Not for our railways was anything like the scene in Charlie Chaplin's film *The Great Dictator* when 'Hitler's' train stopped at the wrong spot for the red carpet.

In spite of a conflict of loyalties, steam enthusiasts were delighted when, on the first occasion Her Majesty's train was entrusted to diesel power, the engine broke down and one of the stand-by steam engines had to come to the rescue. The voluminous instructions issued for each Royal Train journey were naturally very matter-of-fact in tone. One give-away to the patriotic fervour of their compilers could be seen in one of the last Royal Train notices issued by the old Great Western. At the end, emotion got the better of the compiler, leading to a rare split infinitive in the final 'ALL CONCERNED TO SPECIALLY NOTE . . .'.

If, perhaps, the railways give absolute priority to royalty, their good customers can also get rather special service. One recalls an incident of some twenty years ago concerning a firm whose name is a household word and who every quarter wrote B.R. a cheque well into seven figures in the pounds of those days. They were launching a new agricultural product with a jamboree at their works for *their* best customers; it was to include two special trains, one from London and one from elsewhere, coming right into the factory – their business was such that normally a freight train ran in or out every fifteen minutes or so. Every few days the sales manager rang B.R. headquarters to ask if there would be water in the lavatories, and at one meeting this writer was asked what would happen if the special derailed on their lines. He could only reply that as B.R. was bringing the train 230 miles from London and they had to take it only 230 yards, really the thing to do was not to worry too much. Alas, they did worry too much, refastening and renewing their permanent way until everything was bottle-tight and communicating some of this worry to B.R., with the result that an equally bottle-tight ex-works locomotive was put on the job. The combination had not quite enough flexibility, with the result that on the great day the train came slowly in through the factory gates and promptly (and gently) the leading pair of wheels became derailed. In the end the firm took comfort from the idea that the day would have been a memorable one anyway for their customers (who were not seriously incommoded); with this added bonus, it had been one never to be forgotten.

The gradual disappearance of steam has been the excuse for hundreds of special trains. These have ranged from a one-coach steam train with 0–4–2 tank engine on the 3-mile Wallingford branch in Berkshire, to a ten-day, 1,500-mile trip on a special sleeping- and dining-car train covering a major circuit of Southern Africa, using successively fourteen different types of steam locomotive, all highly polished for the occasion. Since this book is all about the pleasures of railways, may one say that these trips (which still continue) offer the highest order of railway enjoyment at a surprisingly reasonable cost.

Imagine rolling down in the early evening to a place called Mossel Bay behind an enormous polished black Garratt locomotive called *Amin* (I called the engine that because it is *big, black* and *cantankerous*, said the driver), then being shunted into a siding alongside the Indian Ocean. One was then able to climb down from one's sleeping car on to the beach and run into the surf. While in South Africa your author was asked by a friend at home to look up his son and daughter, who lived in one of the places this 'Sunset Limited' train was to be stabled at. All the way down Africa he rehearsed the speech: 'Your father asked me to have a word with you – why not come and have a drink on my train? It's stabled in the station.' But, alas, this rather super bit of oneupmanship did not come off, as the youngsters were away. Incidentally, in addition to a lounge/bar car, there was a special lounge car at the front for tape-recorders. While some never seemed to leave the former, one friend never failed to be operating in the latter even when exceptionally the train kept rolling all night or set off in the small hours. What a relief, too, to be spared the packing and unpacking, the booking in and out of hotels, as well as the hazards of over-sleeping. It was also rather pleasant to watch the motorcade of photographers who followed the train all round the country in the dust and heat; particularly so when enjoying a cool glass of wine in the air-conditioned comfort of the buffet car.

Other delights of the 'Sunset Limited' included good company with some long-lost old friends as well as new ones; perhaps the finest railway spectacle was the ascent to the 5,727-foot summit of the Lootsberg Pass, with two 4–8–2s making wonderful exhaust music and a 2–8–4 pushing away hard at the rear. They even managed a run-past.

Although run by South African Railways, the 'Sunset Limited' was organized by the Railway Society of Southern Africa. South African Railways themselves also run similar and rather more frequent trips known as Steam Safaris – their office in Leicester Square, London, will no doubt provide details.

Steam specials began in Britain way back in 1938 when the London & North Eastern Railway, an organization which was given to conducting its affairs with a certain panache, launched some very plush new trains for its crack 'Flying Scotsman' express. They were teak-built and teak-finished and were of the kind that gave rise to that definition of a vintage car: 'When you shut the door it should sound like shutting the door of a first-class carriage on the pre-war Flying Scotsman.' But at King's Cross the press party were ushered into a train of old but clean six-wheelers hauled by the undoubtedly lovely although rather long-funnelled Stirling No. 1 4–2–2 from York Museum. It was of course the 'Flying Scotsman' of 1888, shortly before bogie carriages, corridors and dining cars arrived on the scene; in this cortège the press party settled down to Stevenage, where a gleaming spit-new luxury train awaited them. Hearing of this the Railway Correspondence and Travel Society chartered the oldies for a run to Cambridge and back, thereby to some extent making history.

In Britain, as almost every class of locomotive, steam or otherwise, gets withdrawn from service, groups such as the R.C. and T.S., the Stephenson Locomotive Society and the Locomotive Club of Great Britain either severally or together charter specials for their members to have a final run. In fact, famous locomotives have made as many consecutive last appearances as the most reluctant-to-stand-down actors or actresses. Even now that they are all in museums, they still appear out on the main line, their admirers filling the trains they haul and blanketing the hillsides along the run. One of the things that passengers in these specials enjoy is this almost royal progress through the countryside, watched by the crowds of 'gricers', whose antics never fail to please. Some also impress, as we shall see in the next chapter.

9 · WATCHING THE TRAINS GO BY

Hector and *Ajax* meet, their speeds at par,
Short time for greeting, none at all for war.

ANON., from *The Stuffed Owl*
An Anthology of Bad Verse

It could be said that this is where all train-lovers began – if they were lucky while they were still in their prams. From watching the trains go by we can graduate to recording their numbers, taking their pictures, making models of them, becoming expert in their nuts-and-bolts, or even running them ourselves. But sensible railway enthusiasts never forget what is the very basis of their enthusiasm – the sight and sound of a moving train. Or, better still, two fast-running ones (even now it could be *Hector* and *Ajax*) passing at speed nearby.

Without doubt the king of the train watchers is distinguished photographer Henry Casserley, who, when he set up a home, had it built close to the Euston to Crewe main line. The instruction given to the architect was that the occupants must be able to see the trains from every room in the house, including the smallest; and so it is, the feat being assisted by a curve in the line at the place in question. If his pleasure in the passing scene is reduced now that the uniformity of electrification has replaced the variety of steam, it is enhanced by the lucky escape he had one morning in 1952 when, by chance and quite exceptionally, he was unwell. His train to work was almost completely destroyed in the tragic triple collision at Harrow.

Which brings one to another point about watching trains.

Apart from the actual sight and sound of the train rushing by, the pleasure seems to owe something to the unfolding of a well-ordered routine occasionally seasoned with the unexpected. On this particular tragic day your author raised his eyes from some survey work on the Great Western line just south of Birmingham only to see a Blackpool to Euston express go by. It was like encountering a London omnibus in the middle of New York.

For a young train-watcher the age of innocence – when he is just content to enjoy what he sees and hears – soon passes and he has to move on to recording, that is, to taking down engine numbers. Number-taking – 'spotting' it used to be called – flourishes just as well by the lineside as it does in termini and loco depots. The number-taking king of England was the late Richard Walford, who collected not only engine numbers but coach and wagon numbers as well. The writer, who often went train-watching with this man during his short life, never failed to wonder as Richard began writing down numbers without looking down at the page when the first wagon of the train came near enough. Of course, as the train passed, the writing-down got further and further behind, and even when the brake van of a fifty-wagon goods train was out of sight round the bend, the Walford pencil would still be writing down the long queue of five- and six-figure numbers, complete with prefixes, held in his amazing memory – plus, of course, a cipher for wagon description, for even though the British wagon fleet has fallen from over a million in number to a mere 200,000 or so, neither then nor now do published booklets of wagon numbers exist.

After graduating as a 'spotter', most enthusiasts move on to photography. Here it must be said that the photography of moving trains is not the easiest of arts even for experts. Samuel Butler defined genius as the 'supreme capacity for taking trouble'. Nowhere is this better illustrated than in that superb picture book on South African Railways, *The Great Steam Trek* (Hamlyn, 1978), a book which set new standards for this the most popular form of railway literature. The authors, Alan Jorgenson and Charles Lewis, like all the top train photographers, got their pictures by taking pains, waiting for hours (sometimes days) for a single shot, getting up before dawn, putting up with endless disappointments and finally discarding all but the very best.

As the 'Sunset Limited' (mentioned in the previous chapter) wound its elegant way round Southern Africa, these merchants, plus a cortège of others, could be seen over and over again tearing past on rough dusty bush roads. Equally frequently they would be come across firing off some extremely heavy camera artillery from step-ladder grandstands mounted on the roofs of their vans. Their armoury also included bush-cutting tools to enable landscapes to be altered to the photographers' satisfaction.

A conversation during one of those rare moments when both the 'Sunset Limited' train and its photographic cortège were at rest in the same place at the same time elicited the fact that the trouble taken to approach perfection in railway photography included a dummy run the previous week. This covered the whole route from Johannesburg via Kimberley to Port Elizabeth, across to Mossel Bay and returning via the Lootsbert Pass and Bloemfontein.

For those who, while they enjoy watching trains, prefer to do so when they like rather than when the train likes, home movies are an excellent way of recording trains, especially now that sound cameras and film are generally available. One might easily come back from a fortnight's train chasing with 800 feet of exposed film, which might when cut give a thirty-minute performance. It is bad enough perhaps that the film stock itself would cost over £100, but if one ever decided to defray expenses by selling copies professionally, £50 might just pay for the material used in the copying. With marketing costs and a modest reward for one's trouble, the film could hardly be sold at less than £100, which is really too much for more than a very small sale. On the other hand a cheap portable convenient video recorder can only be a few years away, and the equivalent cost of the tape needed then would be under £5 instead of £100. A pessimist

1. One of the world's greatest junctions – Newcastle-upon-Tyne. A special train hauled by preserved 4–6–2 *Bittern* is leaving for Edinburgh.

2. Edwardian perfection: the blue and gold of a 'Claud Hamilton' class 4–4–0.

3. 'March Forward' class 2–10–0 steam locomotive under construction at Datong, China, November 1980. Production averages 320 per year.

4. A life-long railway enthusiast observes a Darjeeling–Himalayan mountain-climbing locomotive with pleasure and absorption.

5. Xuzhou locomotive shed, China. 'March Forward' class 2–10–2 QJ 3099 (Datong Works, 1979) in the foreground.

6 (*above*). A 'baby-crocodile' vintage electric locomotive moves through the snow near Davos on the metre-gauge Rhaetian Railway of Switzerland.

7 (*left*). Disc-type signal on the Rhaetian Railway of Switzerland.

8 (*opposite*). British signalling: the down goods home signal at Guisborough Junction, Middlesborough.

9. Rolling along: preserved 'Castle' class 4–6–0 No. 5051 *Drysllwyn Castle* climbing Hatton Bank in Warwickshire.

10.. Two 2-foot gauge 2–8–2s hauling the South African Railways' 'Apple Express' tourist train from Port Elizabeth to Loerie draw forward to take water at an intermediate stop.

11. The South African Railways' 'Sunset Limited' safari train stabled overnight in the docks at Port Elizabeth.

12. A special train organized by the Illini Railway Club of Chicago pauses at Chama, New Mexico, on the Denver and Rio Grande Western Railroad. Note the snow plough mounted on the locomotive.

13. Watching the trains go by. An admiring crowd enjoys the passage of a class 'WP' 4–6–2 south of Agra, India.

14. Locomotive enthusiasts visiting the metre-gauge shed at Delhi, India.

might say it rather looks as though the ideal way of recording the steam engine will become effectively available at about the time it finally becomes extinct as a commercial transport tool.

Of course many professional railway movies have been made, and here the video revolution has already engulfed us, since *non*-portable, convenient and fairly reasonably priced video recorders can be easily set up at home and (although it would be naughty to offer the results for sale) pictures of trains come pouring into the home by virtue of our television services. Even when measured by the railway-lovers' criterion – percentage of train time to other time – these still have no rival in the world.

Equally with no rival in the world as a train movie (and recently on our T.V. screens) is Jean Renoir's *La Bête Humaine*, made in 1938; never has the thrill of steam train movement been so well captured. Jean Gabin, who starred, with Simone Simon as the *femme fatale*, apparently fulfilled a lifetime's ambition by having to learn to drive a steam locomotive. There is a shot taken from the tender of picking up water from the troughs between the rails, with Gabin in sole charge on the footplate – it could not possibly have been faked. Auntie B.B.C. gave us the soft version where at the end, after the driver had knocked out his fireman and jumped to his death, the fireman recovers and brings the train to a stand. There exists also a version, closer to Émile Zola's original novel, in which the crowded train races on uncontrolled to its final doom.

But *La Bête Humaine* is only one of 800 railway films referred to in John Huntley's *Railways in the Cinema* (Ian Allan, 1969). The coming of video cannot but have brought closer to the ordinary individual this splendid way of watching trains that have already gone by.

IO · IRON HORSE

... then we came to the long bank up to Tring. It was now dark and the old *Auditor* going all out was a sight I shall ever remember – the top of the chimney looked like what I should imagine Mount Vesuvius looked like in the last days of Pompeii; red, orange and blue flames.

'L.B.S.C.', 'Shops, Shed & Road'
(from the *Model Engineer*)

Driving or even riding on a fast well-found locomotive is a railway pleasure which few people other than professionals will have a chance of enjoying; even the professionals are liable to get an overdose, so that much of *their* pleasure is lost. In Britain one can sit close behind the driver of a diesel multiple-unit train and in this way it is possible to get the feel of driving most current types of motive power by merely buying an ordinary ticket. Steam locomotives are more difficult, but ways of getting to drive one, as well as an amateur's view of what it feels like, are described in *How to Drive a Steam Locomotive*. Professional accounts of firing and driving steam locomotives are now quite common and these also give railway lovers a chance to enjoy the pleasures of driving in a vicarious way. A very good account of engine-driving by an amateur but concerning a professional is Peter Semmens' *Engineman Extraordinary*, the biography of Bill Hoole of King's Cross, the hero of many fine runs on the line to Peterborough, Doncaster and stations north. One last trip that did not appear therein was that of a special train taking a distinguished press party to the opening of the then new electrification from Sheffield to Manchester. A polished streamlined class A4 Pacific gave them two maxima over 100 mph on the smooth and rapid journey down to Sheffield, after which the jolting trundle (at a maximum speed of 60 mph because of problems concerned with the effect of electric locomotives on the track) over to Manchester gave the journalists some doubt as to which type of traction was replacing which to make a better and more modern railway.

On one occasion during the time the biography was being written, Bill Hoole was brought to try his hand on a certain $3\frac{1}{2}$-inch-gauge railway, one on which my seven-year-old daughter was very competent at driving. I regret to say that she was rather apt to offer instruction to her father's friends. Bill was particularly delighted to be told how to drive a steam locomotive by a seven-year-old girl and, charming fellow that he was, pressed half-a-crown into a hot little hand on leaving. I am not sure that before this she had ever realized that money existed in such large amounts.

As regards footplate-riding for the ordinary person, it was just a little easier on Bill Hoole's favourite type of locomotive because some of the L.N.E.R. streamline 4–6–2s had corridor tenders. These were provided in order to allow the changing of engine crews *en route* during the world's longest non-stop run – the 393 miles from London to Edinburgh. It did also mean that one could walk through the train on to the footplate. Of course, one could also leave the footplate this way and this was helpful, for the vibration, the noise, the heat of the fire on one side, the cold and the wind on the other, were too much for some people after more than a minute or two. So a visitor could be invited on to the engine with much less of a commitment. Normally British Railways and its predecessors would meet requests for footplate passes only in very special circumstances.

Private owners of steam locomotives which run main-line excursions on B.R. have a footplate ride for one person at a time in their gift, as it were. However, it is customary to reserve this place for those who have given freely of their time to maintaining the locomotive, so for outsiders there is little chance. Of course, the problem is that British cabs are cramped, the engine crew need room to work and a locomotive inspector always travels on the engine, so only one supernumerary can be accommodated.

As one might expect, footplate rides, both official and unofficial, are easier to come by in foreign countries. Most Indian locomotive drivers, for example, are amenable to a polite request to ride with them. There is ample room on a huge broad-gauge footplate for the crew of four as well as *two* visitors, and exciting it certainly is, especially at night. A total experience, you could say, as you go tearing through the warm Indian night on a rollicking, roaring, vibrating locomotive, with the headlight boring a path ahead into the darkness and a competent crew tending the huge furnace and watching for signal lights ahead.

On the other hand in Africa it is a little more difficult, though still far easier than in Britain. In steam days in Kenya, footplate rides were usually offered to visitors with only modestly convincing reasons for getting one, but it had to be done officially and well in advance, at least on the main line anywhere near the bows of the flagship. An occasion when I was allowed to blow that elephant-scaring whistle to clear some ostriches off the track ahead of a 252-ton monster Beyer-Garratt is one that will forever stay in the memory. Rhodesia (and Zimbabwe will probably not be very different) also had a railway system where an approach to officialdom usually produced results.

South Africa is a country where young men from Britain can and do go firing steam locomotives, in rather the same way as the adventurous 1930s generation used to go to the Åland Islands in the Baltic to join the last few of the big sailing ships for voyages home with grain from Australia. Firing locomotives is a hard life, but at least those who try it are taking the very last opportunity in the world of doing something that is a real man's job and an exciting one to boot.

It is a curious thing about some communist countries that a

ride on the engine is no problem, but taking a photograph of it means immediate arrest by the police. I do not by this suggest that an official approach to the railway administration would produce results in getting a ride on the locomotive – or for that matter obtaining permission to take pictures of it, this being a matter for the state security police rather than for the railway authorities. Instead, provided that one can accept a refusal, the memorizing of some suitable phrase in the vernacular such as 'Please can I ride with you on your steam locomotive?' does surprisingly often produce results.

Occasionally it can do more than that. On a remote line in Greece, an English couple made a similar request and climbed on to the engine. They were made so welcome and enjoyed the sensations of the ride so much that they went on beyond the point from where it was possible that night to return to the place at which they were staying. On arrival at the terminus the driver insisted that they stay the night with him, but it wasn't a restful one because his neighbours in this little town of Milai, well outside the tourism belt, came round to meet what were to them visitors from outer space. The party lasted almost until train time the next morning. But this was a narrow-gauge country and traditionally things are less formal in places where the rails are nearer together.

Royal locomotive riders have not been unknown. Of course, there are ceremonial episodes like the one which resulted in the commemorative plate fixed to Great Western locomotive No. 4082 *Windsor Castle*. This indicated that the locomotive had been driven from Swindon Station as far as the factory by King George V when he visited the railway works in 1926. And there are the engine rides which have come the way of royal children, such as Prince Charles's ride on the Romney, Hythe & Dymchurch Railway some twenty-five years ago, or that of one of Princess Margaret's children more recently on the Festiniog line.

But there have also been grown-up Royals who rode and drove locomotives. King Boris of Bulgaria was the most famous. It is even said that the palace in Sofia dictated certain aspects of locomotive policy; the fact that during King Boris's reign the State Railways acquired 4–10–0s and 2–12–4 tank locomotives – both of them unique types – lends support to this view. But it is certainly true that Boris of Bulgaria often drove locomotives; on one occasion he stepped into the breach in an emergency when his saloon was attached to a public train and the driver was hurt by a blow-back from the fire.

Alfonso, the pre-war King of Spain, had a cousin who drove locomotives on the Spanish Railways. This Spanish grandee also insisted on driving his royal relative personally whenever the Spanish monarch travelled abroad. Once at the end of a state visit to France, with protracted farewells going on between the King of Spain and the President of the Republic, a grimy figure leaned from the locomotive cab and said, 'For God's sake get a move on Alfonso, we're late already.'

11 · IRON ROAD

Long before the day of the first railway
locomotive, the first railway track had come
into use.

CECIL J. ALLEN, *The Steel Highway*

So far each chapter in this book has dealt with an aspect of
railway-loving which is the first interest of a substantial number
of enthusiasts. One that is usually not a major interest is, oddly
enough, the matter of the tracks themselves; and yet everything
involved in making and looking after this iron road (more
correctly, this steel highway) is fascinating to a degree which
makes the majority of the professionals also enthusiasts. Something of the spirit of the game was mentioned in the introduction,
while most of the technology can be found in *British Permanent
Way*, published by the Permanent Way Institution.

Your author looks back on seventeen pleasurable years spent
fairly close to British railway track. I don't mean that every day
was unalloyed enjoyment – imagine 3 am on a winter's morning
in a draughty spot, snow falling hard and almost horizontally,
contemplating a hole which had to be made into a railway in time
for the first train at 8 am. Also, while personal responsibility for
the safe running of trains, all the way down the chain of
command from Chief Engineer to ganger, gave a considerable
immunity from the types of interference which are a hazard of
other less responsible jobs, it also meant a great deal of anxiety
from time to time. However, once one moved on and up to so-
called higher things, the relief of not having to sign statements
such as 'I certify that the Down line between Eryholme and Croft

is now fit for the passage of trains at 80 mph' was apt to lead to a slightly casual attitude towards signing the bits of administrative paper put before one in the new job.

In Dr Beeching's time the mileage of railway track (and hence, in proportion, the number of responsible engineers' posts) suddenly shrank from 19,000 to 11,000, so many of us had perforce to move on to other things. A colleague, rather sad at having to give up a lifetime's ambition to get one of the key (and now almost vanished) posts of District Engineer, said 'I'd have liked to have been a District Engineer. There's only one difference between God and a District Engineer and that is the size of his district.'

There was a certain District Engineer who, overmindful I'm afraid of his high status, was given to uttering Latin tags at Inspectors' meetings. This author, who served under him for a short while, perhaps rather naïvely once capped one of these with one of the few he happened to know, this by chance being appropriate. It was the end of Latin as a means of communication on this sector of B.R., although American railroads still use it in speaking of the *per diem* payments for one road's cars being used by another.

Even Assistant District Engineers were issued with permanent footplate passes and were *expected* in the days of steam to use them regularly. At Darlington the district ran from Northallerton to Durham, places at which the fastest trains did not stop, so the pass covered York to Newcastle. There were also strenuous but pleasant days out in the Inspection Saloon, which compensated for other occasions when one put in twenty-four anxious hours at a stretch at a weekend without overtime pay.

The Darlington district also extended over the Pennines via Stainmore Summit, a route notorious for becoming blocked by snow. In 1947 the line had been blocked for weeks by drifts that extended as high as the eaves of buildings. A film called *Snowdrift on Bleath Gill* was made, which is excellent, but by the time the filmers got up there the snow had thawed somewhat and those engaged on shovelling it were asked to kneel down so it should seem deeper. When snow came to Stainmore in your author's time there, he was determined not to allow the line to become blocked and so scheduled frequent ploughings to avoid it. All was well and the line stayed open; but when the weather improved he did just wonder why there was no word of thanks from the traffic department. On inquiry, however, it appeared that so many locomotives and crews were used in keeping the line free of drifts, there was none left to haul traffic!

The sight of a big wedge plough, propelled by three or four steam locomotives, charging a snowdrift at full speed is one of the great railways sights of the world. The effort put into the otherwise superb film *Murder on the Orient Express* was feeble compared to the real thing; but the makers were hampered by the fact that the winter when it was made turned out to be an almost snow-less one. Snow had to be trucked in to make the drift in which the train was 'stuck'.

Another of the great railway sights of the world was, as already mentioned, the picking-up of water on the run. Fairly tiresome to the engineering staff at any time were the sets of water troughs, but during a spell of arctic weather they were murder. You could say that the locomotives taking water created their own freezing rain, and soon some real North Pole landscape would be created; you needed special spiked boots on the resulting glacier even to inspect the lines. The troughs have no ends and people often wonder by what magic the water is made to stay in them. The answer is that a short gradient is formed at each end so that the track is lower over the main middle length of the troughs than it is at either end. The Lancashire & Yorkshire railway, which had a surprisingly large number of water troughs considering its rather compact route system, gave the trick away by erecting gradient posts to mark these short down-gradients of perhaps 150 feet in length.

Talking of lineside posts, train-lovers who relied on mile-posts for their timings would have even less confidence in their results if they had known of one of the permanent-way inspectors on the Darlington district. This gentleman had been known to dig up a mile-post and bring it a little closer in, in order that a length of track he was proposing for renewal would seem longer than it actually was. Of course, he would then be issued with extra material ...

Perhaps enough has been said to show that there was a good deal of fun to be had in what was a very serious and exacting occupation, but there were other aspects which of themselves had the elements of pleasure. The exercise of particular and remarkable skills is one of them. It is fairly hard to believe, for example, that hefty rails $5\frac{1}{2}$ inches high and $2\frac{3}{4}$ inches wide can be cut using a hammer and sett or chisel unless one has seen it done, though I think the practice is frowned on nowadays. First one marked the rail right round with the hammer and chisel. The rail was then given a tiny squeeze with a 'Jim Crow', a device used for bending rails, and finally it was hit hard with a large hammer, when the two halves just fell apart nice and square ready to be drilled for fishplates.

A similar delight is the joining of rails *in situ* by welding. After preparation, cleaning, setting up a mould, preheating etc., one arranges a kind of casting pot just above the joint and puts into it a mixture known as 'thermit'. This is ignited, when it goes off like a Roman candle many times life-size, finally leaving the pot full of white-hot molten iron. The pot is then tapped and the weld metal streams down into the mould, forming, if all goes well, a weld strong enough to stand the appalling stresses and vibrations of heavy traffic.

One is often asked, now that welded rails are used, how natural expansion is catered for in long lengths of continuously welded rail where there are no expansion spaces between adjacent rails at joints. The answer is that the forces trying to expand or contract the rail through heat or cold are held as a stress in the metal. This stress is kept within bounds by making sure that when the rails are laid and fastened down, they are at a mean temperature, that is, halfway between hot and cold. Welded track is also very heavily ballasted and also nowadays involves concrete sleepers, which are much heavier than timber ones. In these ways the forces induced by changes of temperature are not only held within bounds, but buckling in hot weather is prevented.

Another aspect of the permanent way which could even rank as an art rather than a skill is the design of railway layouts. First one makes a survey out on the ground, which is then plotted. Then one has to resolve all the conflicting requirements and limitations, as well as incorporate any changes necessary, either because traffic has altered or different material is to be used, for instance flat-bottom rails in place of bull-head. Then one way or another one has to ensure that all the fittings are actually put down on the ground in the place the designer intended. Finally, of course, if all goes well, one has the considerable pleasure of seeing one's junction with all its voluptuous curves and crossings become an intrinsic part of Britain's network of rails. And even if one has only done a little bit of this sort of work, perhaps only in model form, the experience gained gives an ability to appreciate the art involved in producing fine-looking railway layouts.

Without doubt the most complex – and judge for yourself if it is not also the most artistic – junction layout in the world is that at the north end of Newcastle-upon-Tyne Central Station. It involves diamond crossings, all of them being not only different but of the most complex kind geometrically. By this I mean that, owing to the opposing curvature, the individual angles at the four corners of each diamond are also different.

At this point (please excuse the pun) we break surface into the sunshine of a world in which numerous railway-lovers take pleasure. Instead of seeing complex railway layouts as intersecting pairs of rails supported by timbers and sleepers whose claim to being an art form lies in the geometrical shapes involved, these layout enthusiasts see a network of *tracks*, whose pretensions towards being art lie in their properties as networks. As so often is the case, the existence of books underlines the strength of interest in this particular aspect of the hobby. Here we salute the dedication of R. A. Cooke of Harwell, Oxfordshire, who has begun a series of books of historical and present-day layout diagrams which, starting in the south-west, is no doubt intended to extend to the rest of Britain. Perhaps one-fifth of the country has been covered in the thirty-eight separate titles so far issued. Books about railways could hardly be more basic than these.

12 · SCULPTURE IN THE LANDSCAPE

Henceforth old Tamar will be spanned by its double ferruginous bow, presenting with Cyclopean triumph a grand highway of commerce across the broad bosom of the waters.

ANON. (*a journalist enjoys himself describing Brunel's new bridge across the River Tamar at Saltash near Plymouth*)

Great was the uproar when the early railway builders began to cut scars into the hillsides. There were predictions that sheep and cattle would be made barren, crops would fail and fruit wither on the trees. On the whole none of this has happened, except perhaps when the sheep and cattle get frightened, the crops trampled and the fruit picked by railway-lovers finding vantage points to watch the trains go by. Nowadays the shock has long vanished, railway works and structures being very much the in-thing to admire even in the wide world outside railway enthusiast circles.

Buildings, even the greatest, have always seemed to this writer to be lumpish kinds of things, but bridges are something else again. From the largest ones such as the Forth Bridge across an arm of the sea north of Edinburgh, to a humble stone arch taking a farm track across a country branch line, their shape and appearance have always had an appeal which could not be ignored.

Other railway constructions have claims to being worth looking at – for example, the great overall roofs that some large stations have, which stun the senses with their magnificence. At the other end of the scale is the country station, whose buildings are too small to be lumpish, and where the care lavished on etceteras like flower beds by a staff who tended to have time on their hands between infrequent trains enhances any cottagy beauty they may possess. Each has its counterpart of horror – the verandah roofs typical of moderate-sized stations are very difficult to make into something that is a pleasure to look at, however elaborate the pattern cut into their valances might be; while the country station which has been 'rationalized' by means of a not-quite-complete demolition of nice buildings and their replacement by pre-fabricated and vandalized shelters is something to which it is better to shut one's eyes.

Tunnels are certainly superb achievements, but by very definition they remain hidden from view. A total respect for those who earn a perilous living by making or maintaining holes in the earth, learnt during a period of personal involvement, has not left room for any liking for the objects of their toil.

Having had all these things in mind as being part of a good way of life, there came a day in the summer of 1946 when, clutching his slide rule and a box of drawing instruments, your author entered the office of the Chief Engineer – the fifth since Brunel – of the Great Western Railway. But, alas no, it was not a scheme for a replacement double-track Saltash Bridge which was put on his desk for execution, but piles of prints to be coloured with draughtsman's water colours. Hooker's Green, Payne's Grey, Brick Red and Prussian Blue were the order of the day and, while the syllabus in the Cambridge Engineering Schools had not concerned itself with such archaic practices, fortunately a kindergarten teacher fifteen years before had grounded her pupils well in putting on colour washes ... A hundred or so elephant-sized drawings looked very nice when they were finished! But it was not too long before some potential new bridges did come along to be surveyed, drawn out and, finally coloured.

A *Good Bridge Guide* would hardly be needed to tell of something that might reasonably be taken for granted, since bridges that fail to do their job are rare even by the severe standards of railway safety; this in spite of one or two spectacular collapses such as that of the Scottish Tay Bridge in 1879. On the other hand our *Beautiful Bridge Brochure* would be nice but almost useless to travellers by train, because one thing that railway passengers do not usually get an opportunity to do is to admire the proportions of the structures their train passes across. Occasionally this inability to see bridges from trains extends to a rather disconcerting total invisibility; this was common after the war in Europe, where emergency rebuilding allowed solely for supporting the rails and nothing for parapets, railings and refuges. This simple and cheap form of railway bridge is also fairly common in what are now politely referred to as the developing nations.

It would be difficult to argue a case for any other than the arched bridge to be awarded the top prizes in the bridge beauty stakes. The suspension bridge – whose mathematics are very similar, except that everything is upside down and the thrust in the voussoir stones of the arch is replaced by the pull in the cables – is too lively under concentrated loads to be really suitable for railway trains. Girder bridges have to be very large indeed to become impressive, and this certainly also goes for trestle bridges, whether of steel or timber. But designing a mean or ugly arch is near enough impossible.

Up until now, except briefly when talking of steam loco-motives, we have not talked of beauty but concerned ourselves with enjoyment. Beauty and its appreciation are a very serious kind of pleasure but none the less absorbing for that. But how to describe looks in words, that is the problem. Even photographs are only a beginning; the sculpture implicit in providing an effective railway grade over inconvenient terrain can only be admired by an expedition in the field. So, readers, off with your slippers, out of your armchair, on with your anorak and Wellington boots – you will find the rewards worthwhile.

13 · ACCIDENT AND INCIDENT

Casey Jones! Mounted to the cabin
Casey Jones! with his orders in his hand
Casey Jones! Mounted to the cabin
Took his farewell trip to the Promised Land

ANON., American railroad song

It is probably because the insides of railway trains are amongst the safest places in the world that when accidents happen they attract enormous attention from media and public. If in Britain there was only a million to one chance of being killed on a railway journey, then over 1,000 passengers would be killed every year on the trains. In fact, an average of twenty or so is the figure. The dangers inherent in air travel are five times as great and thus still negligible; however, the private car is five times more risky still, that is, twenty-five times as dangerous as a train and thus its risks are very far from being negligible. It certainly should be one of the pleasures of travelling by rail that, however much the carriage may rock, vibrate, jar or sway, the chances of a sticky end being in store for the traveller are incredibly remote.

The reasons for this satisfactory state of affairs are far from being happy ones, however; the measures that ensure safety on the world's railways were born not out of far-sightedness but in death and destruction. The Gods certainly had it in mind to teach presumptuous mortals a lesson when they essayed the annihilation of time and space with fire chariots running at mind-boggling speeds of 30 mph or so. Day One of Inter-City Travel – 15 September 1830 – was marred by the death of William

Huskisson, M.P., who stepped in front of a moving train. Before another year had gone by, the fireman of *Best Friend of Charleston* tied down the safety valve and that was the second recorded fatality – and this led to safety valves which could not be tampered with except by means of special tools. One might again cite the famous accident at Harrow in October 1952 when the deaths of 108 people led to the installation of a cab signalling system in Britain – except on the lines of the old Great Western Railway, which had had it for many years before.

You may well ask how these grim matters come into a book on the *pleasures* of railways. Of course, there were railway accidents which were undiluted pleasure even for those concerned. I often think of a major freight train derailment (with no one hurt) on the London to Edinburgh main line south of Darlington. A large (and untypical) Yorkshire farmer dressed in pyjamas and carrying a shot-gun was not at all disposed to allow us access to the scene across his land; but when Operating Superintendent Ted McClelland said 'Do you realize you are delaying Her Majesty's Mails?', instant collapse of farmer took place with obvious visions of accommodation at the Tower of London. In fact the train contained (amongst other things) chocolates rather than mail, and it is fairly doubtful whether one can demand passage even for the Royal Mail over someone else's fields in the middle of the night, but the trick worked. Later, when we were on the scene wading ankle-deep in chocolates, the breakdown crane driver unwrapped and ate one, only to be promptly arrested by the railway police for looting. After some argument the course of justice was perverted sufficiently so that the job of clearing the line could continue.

Even when the consequences of an accident were serious or even gruesome, lighter moments sometimes enlivened the subsequent inquiries. There was the driver of a Leeds to London express whose steed left the rails not far out of London. He miraculously escaped (although not all his passengers did) and described how he felt the engine roll just before the accident: 'So

I said to her, "steady, old girl", but she went over too far to recover.'

One writer of detective stories, Freeman Wills Crofts, who had also been a professional railway engineer, gave some very authentic details of railway accident procedure in his novel *Death of a Train*. Other writers, less conversant with the reality of what goes on behind the scenes on the railway, have dealt with railway accidents sensationally but with scant regard for realism. The enjoyment of a sense of superiority over some well-known best-selling novelist is of course a real source of pleasure to a knowledgeable railway enthusiast. It is like that story by 'Saki' (H. H. Munro) where the little boy refuses to eat his porridge on the grounds that there was a baby frog in it (he had put it there himself) and the grown-ups expressed themselves forcibly that it was impossible. He got into serious trouble, but the facet of the incident that impressed the little boy most was the fact that his elders and betters had stated something very firmly and had been proved to be profoundly in the wrong. The worrying thing is (and it applies most particularly to the media) that if they get the wrong end of the stick over something one knows about, how can one put even the smallest faith in other things upon which they pontificate?

Private inquiries are always held by the railway into incidents which, while often both startling and worrying, do not lead to serious injury. They have to be reported to the Ministry if any passenger train was or could have been involved. For example, something hanging from a locomotive once got caught in the end of a short check rail. This became lifted out of its chairs and, since the train was going very fast, the check rail rose and passed up diagonally through the compartments of the leading carriages. Fortunately the train was not full and injuries were confined to one small boy who had his leg broken, but it must have been fairly startling for those involved. The incident occurred on the Southern Region main line between Salisbury and Exeter.

On another rather remarkable occasion, a L.N.E.R. streamline

4–6–2 broke a connecting rod close to its little end, near Thirsk in Yorkshire. The rod dropped, caught in a sleeper and the locomotive jumped over it as it went round. Incredibly the locomotive dropped back on to the rails and just as incredibly the carriages rode over the badly buckled track.

Inquiries held to ascertain the cause are one of the ways in which the occurrence of one sad accident is used to prevent others. A major accident is looked over at three separate inquiries. First, the railway holds its own. Its findings are then made available for one held by the Department of Transport's Railway Inspectorate. Quite independent of these is the legal inquiry, in the form of a coroner's inquest on the dead; occasionally (very occasionally in Britain) this is followed by criminal proceedings against those held to be responsible. The report of the Inspector has no legal significance; it is made public and can be bought from H.M. Stationery Office, though they do not keep a stock of 'back numbers'. It must be said that the accident reports do make good reading, as unputdownable in some cases as anything written by Agatha Christie or Conan Doyle. They are also highly instructive on the true ways of railways and railwaymen, being full (usually) of the heights of their heroism, devotion and resource as well as (occasionally) the depths of their incompetence, sloth and carelessness. One has only to remember Driver John Axon, G.C., who sacrificed his life to save others when the freight train he was driving near Buxton, Derbyshire, ran away; or Driver Gimbert, G.C., who during the war saved Soham in East Anglia by detaching an already burning ammunition wagon from a train and starting to haul it away from the station. He got just far enough before it went up.

The worst accident in British railway history, the collision which happened in May 1915 at Quintinshill on the Caledonian Railway, a few miles north of Carlisle, cost some 224 lives. It involved some very careless doings on the part of the staff, not to speak of forged signatures in the signal-box register. The inquiry into another one at Castlecary, between Edinburgh and

Glasgow, in 1937 (with thirty-five dead) proved little about what really happened (except that many of those who gave evidence were lying), but it did establish the need for more sophisticated signalling equipment.

At Sutton Coldfield in 1955, a train running at a speed of approximately 60 mph through the station became derailed at a place where there was a permanent speed restriction to 30 mph. On this occasion it was possible to estimate the speed from a photograph taken by a railway enthusiast who was on the spot at the time. The accident took place when the train had been diverted on to another route during engineering operations, a 'conductor' driver being provided to assist the train driver who was unfamiliar with the substitute line. An unsatisfactory feature was that the latter was taking it easy on the cushions in the train contrary to the rules.

In other parts of the world, very similar procedures are followed regarding railway accidents, except that in many of them the police play a much more active role; in Britain criminal proceedings are only resorted to when there has been some really positive criminal negligence. Railways in countries such as India, where British influence was strong, may have changed superficially, but their accident reports (apart from replacing the lion and unicorn on the cover) are still very much carbon copies of those issued by Whitehall. An accident report on a single-line collision in India comes to mind, in which the single-line token for the section concerned had to be recovered with some difficulty from under the pillow of the hospital bed of one of the injured drivers, who was not going to relinquish it without the most clearly worded receipt complete with high-level signature.

The world's two worst railway accidents have both occurred when safety regulations were overruled in the interests of military necessity. A large number of troops were killed, the exact figure being estimated to be in the region of 550, when in December 1917 a train from Italy to France set off down from the Mont Cenis Tunnel. A driver's protests that he had not enough brake power were overruled by the military and the train got out of control, finally derailing on a curve at a speed estimated as being up in the nineties. An overload (but this time uphill) was also blamed for the suffocation of a train-load of passengers near Salerno in Italy in March 1944, the death toll being 530 when the train stalled on an up-gradient in the Armi Tunnel.

The worst recorded railway accident in a country at peace seems to have been in north-eastern Spain, in January 1944; again there were 500 plus deaths, caused by a double collision followed by a fire in a tunnel. But now the matter of records has been raised, let us consider those of a less macabre kind.

14 · RACES AND RECORDS

'Ye'll no be making a long stay in Aberdeen the morn.'

ANON. (*said by a porter to a traveller just arrived from London who immediately got into another train returning there*)

The words above were spoken to journalist (and pioneer train-timer) Charles Rous-Marten at Aberdeen Station in the early morning of a day in July 1895 immediately after the arrival of one of the racing night trains from London. He had rushed across the platform to catch the day train back to London to cover the next night's race. The intention of the contest was to obtain publicity and hence patronage for the victor during the big exodus to the grouse moors for the famous 12 August opening of the shooting season. The long trains necessary to carry this large and lucrative traffic (wives, lady-friends, children, servants, dogs, guns and baggage were involved, as well as the grousers themselves) would preclude any racing during the shooting season itself, but it was felt that sportsmen might prefer to patronize the line which demonstrated the most sporting spirit beforehand.

The west coast and east coast trains started from Euston and King's Cross respectively at 8.0 pm and normally took twelve hours to reach Aberdeen, arriving there in nice time for break-fast. After just a month of racing the time was cut to 8 hours 32 minutes from Euston and 8 hours 40 minutes from King's Cross. Nowadays the H.S.T. 125 from King's Cross does the run in 7 hours 26 minutes, but the night sleeper (also from

King's Cross – there is no service from Euston) still needs nine minutes short of ten hours.

The east coast companies (Great Northern, North Eastern and North British) planned to re-open hostilities in 1896. The N.E.R. actually built a pair of special racing engines with driving wheels of 7 feet 7 inches diameter, but on the west coast the London & North Western Railway lost their appetite for racing after a derailment at Preston during the interim. So actual A-to-B racing came to an end, officially forever, although a little speed competition arose (indeed, still arises) from time to time. Nevertheless the idea of throwing dull timetables to the winds and driving on up to the limit (regardless of safety) thrilled the imagination of the public and turned many a mere harmless ordinary citizen into a railway fanatic.

Among more sedate races that might better be called competition was that in the late 1930s between three great American railroad companies for the passenger business between Chicago and the twin cities of St Paul and Minneapolis. In the summer of 1934 competition began with all three slashing the time for the journey of about 400 miles from ten hours to six and a half. The Chicago & North Western Railway – famous amongst other things for having left-hand running in a drive-on-the-right country and now for belonging to its employees – did it fairly conventionally with its '400' (400 miles in 400 minutes) expresses. The Chicago, Burlington & Quincy Railroad sold the pass and bought a fleet of early diesel streamliners for its 'Zephyr' trains; whereas the Chicago, Milwaukee, St Paul & Pacific Railroad wheeled out some wonderful matching steam locomotives and luxury streamline trains called the 'Hiawathas', the fastest steam expresses ever put into public service.

After accelerations to a $6\frac{1}{4}$-hour timing, which included six stops, the timetable of the 'Hiawatha' involved the fastest start-to-stop run ever scheduled with steam, at 81·5 mph for the seventy-eight miles between Sparta and Portage, Wisconsin. It was also the only schedule where a steam-hauled train needed to exceed 100 mph in order to keep time. Even so, the 'Hiawathas' had something in hand over their rivals, as a proposal for still further acceleration was shelved after the C.&N.W. and C.,B.&Q. had intimated that they were not prepared to follow suit and the three roads had a gentleman's agreement by this time to have equal overall schedules.

It is interesting to compare the Hiawatha trains with the London & North Eastern's contemporary 'Coronation' express, a train of very similar concept:

	Coronation (London– Edinburgh)	Hiawatha (as in 1937) (Chicago–St Paul/ Minneapolis)
Distance	$393\frac{3}{4}$ miles	$411\frac{1}{2}$ miles
Time	6 hrs	$6\frac{1}{4}$ hrs
Average speed	65·3 mph	65·8 mph
No. of stops	2	6
Net time	5 hrs 56 mins.	6 hrs 2 mins.
Net average speed	66·4 mph	68·2 mph
No. of coaches	9	9
Train weight	312 tons (imp.)	382 tons (imp.)
No. of seats	216*	300†
Best wartime schedule (1944)	$8\frac{1}{2}$ hrs	$6\frac{1}{2}$ hrs
Current best time (1981)	4 hrs 52 mins	$8\frac{3}{4}$ hrs

* plus fourteen non-revenue seats in observation car during summer
† plus 199 non-revenue seats in diner and bar

The 4–6–2 on the 'Coronation' could pick up water from troughs at Langley (near Stevenage), Werrington (near Peterborough), Scrooby (near Doncaster), Wiske Moor (near Northallerton) and Lucker (between Newcastle and Berwick), and one suspects that a number of the 'Hiawatha's' six halts were for the purpose of taking water and not for traffic reasons. On the other hand the 'Hiawatha' 4–6–4s could take coal at New Lisbon from a special chute above the tracks in the station. One notes from logs that coaling was done within the three minutes allowed, which may not easily be believed, but the reader is assured from personal observation that U.S. on-line coaling operations were just as quick as that. The 'Coronation' could have done with a quick fuel snack at York – it often ran short of coal further south. While that well-known discovery of Sir Isaac Newton carried the train with steam shut off down the last few miles into King's Cross, it is said that a station pilot had sometimes to haul the now steamless and fireless locomotive back to the shed.

These are the kind of past glories the thoughts of which are certainly one of the great pleasures of railways. There is certainly no problem about finding out the details. Ask any railway enthusiast about railway records and nine out of ten will rattle them off with a facility that clearly indicates their importance to him. Records of speed naturally come first, and several figures apply, so one has to be very careful.

1. Fastest speed ever achieved by a timetabled train in public service: 130 mph, the governed speed applied to numerous trains on the Shin Kansen Railway, Japan.

2. Fastest speed ever achieved by a train on a public railway: 205·7 mph between Bordeaux and Bayonne in France on 28 March 1955. A specially modified electric locomotive was used hauling three coaches.

3. Fastest speed achieved on rails by a vehicle with flanged wheels: 264 mph, by the experimental 'Bertin' train, based on aircraft technology, at Orleans, France, in January 1969.

4. Faster speeds have been achieved on rails experimentally by other forms of rail-guided (but not rail-supported) traction. An

unmanned vehicle supported by magnetic levitation and driven by a linear electric motor has reached 317 mph in Japan.

Our own country has to be content with the record for a timetabled train in public service running independently of any external power source, that is, at the 125 mph (plus a small margin for speedometer error) limit of the famous High Speed Trains.

Of course, the most useful (and therefore least interesting) speed record is that of rail *travel* or start-to-stop running. It seems the Japanese Shin Kansen trains have it firmly in their hands at the moment, as they have had for some time, though by the time this book is in print it will, barring accidents, have passed like the other records into the hands of the French. But both these nations had to build new long-distance railways to achieve the world title (in a commercial sense) for the fastest trains on earth. The Paris–Lyons run, currently an extremely respectable 3 hours 44 minutes for the 318 miles, is coming down to 2 hours for the 265½ miles via the new railway, an average speed start-to-stop of 132 mph and a top speed of 162.

The way in which record speeds have built up to these figures is not known with anything as dull as certainty. But a few mile-stones are clear. The highest speeds in the early days were achieved on the broad-gauge lines of the Great Western and Bristol & Exeter companies. Locomotive Superintendent Daniel Gooch had sufficient confidence to bring H.R.H. Prince Albert back from Bristol to London on 19 July 1843 in an amazing 124 minutes for the 118 miles. In 1847 the G.W.R. 'Flying Dutchman' express to the West was scheduled to run the 52·8 miles from Paddington to Didcot in 55 minutes, reaching Exeter (194 miles) in 4 hours 25 minutes. In 1854, on the Wellington incline in Somerset, an authentic speed of 81·8 mph was recorded behind one of the extraordinary 4–2–4 tank locomotives with 9-foot-diameter wheels of the Bristol & Exeter Railway.

Authentic, ay, there's the rub. Towards the turn of the century various American railroads caught the speed bug and great things were certainly done. The problem is that we don't really know exactly what they were. For example, in 1893, that famous high-stepping 4–4–0 No. 999 of the New York Central Railroad (today preserved in the Chicago Museum of Science and Industry, but with the big 7-foot 2-inch wheels of her giddy youth replaced by smaller workaday ones) was timed by the conductor with an ordinary watch to run a mile in 32 seconds, that is, at 112·5 mph. Alas, since it was an isolated reading not confirmed by other people or by timings taken over adjacent mile sections, No. 999's notable (and more useful) achievement must remain that of bettering the mile-a-minute average between start and stop.

Twelve years later, rival Pennsylvania was talking of start-to-stop runs around 70 mph, plus an equally dubious maximum of 127 mph. In the meantime back in Britain, that prince of train-timers Charles Rous-Marten had on 5 May 1904 timed G.W.R. *City of Truro* 4–4–0 down that same Wellington Bank and claimed a world record speed of 102·3 mph. Alas for British pride, a meticulous analysis of the timings carried out by Cecil J. Allen in the *Railway Magazine* many years ago seemed to indicate that some doubt existed over even this long-accepted figure.

Complete authenticity *was* established for the final steam world speed record, the 126 mph achieved by the London & North Eastern Railway streamline 'A4' class 4–6–2 *Mallard* on 3 July 1938. Two things detracted from this record: considerable assistance was provided by the 1 in 200 down gradient at the location concerned, Stoke Bank, north of Peterborough; and *Mallard*'s works were beginning to disintegrate under the strains involved in turning with such rapid revolutions. A German '05' class 4–6–4, specially built for high speed with 7 foot 6 inch driving wheels, had managed 124·5 mph on 11 May 1936, running on near-level track and without reported ill-effect, hauling a 200-ton test train. The 'Hiawatha' 4–4–2s and 4–6–4s mentioned earlier were also run up to 125 mph on their trials.

Another set of records was set up in 1938 by the performance of one of the Union Pacific Railroad's 'Mighty 800' class of 4–8–4, which on test ran a 1,000-ton passenger train on the level at just over 100 mph, developing some 6,000 hp in the cylinders in order to do so. As well as speeds attained and loads hauled, many other sorts of record performance are recognized. For example, the Northern Pacific Railroad, which scheduled the longest continuous run (of 1,008 miles from Minneapolis to Livingston) for coal-burning steam power, had a record which, having regard to the problems involved, took some earning. But speed remained the principal subject of records.

By the time *City of Truro* had done the ton in 1904, not only had the train already yielded first place to the motor car but even on rails steam had yielded first place to electricity. Some speed trials were held on a fourteen-mile military railway at a place called Zossen, near Berlin. By 1901, 101 mph had been reached and in 1903 an electric railcar built by the A.E.G. Company reached $130\frac{1}{2}$ mph, a record that was to stand for many years. In 1931 an amazing propeller-driven vehicle, also German, managed 143 mph on the Berlin–Hamburg main line. A modern version of this 'Zeppelin' train was improvised by the New York Central Railroad in July 1966, shortly before its disastrous amalgamation with rival Pennsylvania. Two aircraft jet engines mounted on the roof of a modified railcar were used and 183·8 mph was attained. But neither of these two latter ideas had any bearing on the practical transport of people by rail and, of course, the speed of the latter had already been eclipsed by a conventional train in France.

All these records are wonderful to think about and to some extent inspiring for those involved, but it must be said that risks were certainly taken; and had something gone wrong no mercy would have been shown to those whose responsibility it was, even had they survived. Perhaps the most alarming occasion was the press run of the London, Midland & Scottish Railway's new 'Coronation Scot' train from London to Crewe in June 1937. An attempt was made during the descent into Crewe to take the British rail speed record, but someone had not done all the sums appropriate to the amount of energy needed to be dissipated before a train moving downhill at well over 100 mph could be brought to rest. Steam was not shut off until a speed of 113 mph had been reached (it was a tie with the existing record), at a point only two miles south of the station. A full application of the brake seemed to make little difference at first to the speed, until finally No. 6220 stayed on the rails, like the great lady she was, through a series of 20 mph cross-overs leading to the platform line at a speed nearer 60 mph than 20. Crockery crashed in the dining car – but everything else was all right – just. Even so, the imperturbable Driver T. J. Clarke of Camden, after a short rest, then took the party back at a sustained high speed which equalled the present-day electric schedule between Crewe and Euston, showing that at least the footplate staff had not turned a hair over what happened. On the other hand those concerned with the permanent way, who found flange marks on places where wheels are not supposed to be, plus other minor damage indicating the hair's-breadth margin by which disaster was averted, were not quite so easy in their minds.

15 · SHUNTING THE FREIGHT

The total enthusiasts come across a refrigerator car
in a siding in France, read the words 'Not to work
between Finchley Road and Baker Street on the
Metropolitan Railway or between Bo-peep Junction and Tonbridge', and are made helpless by the
crazy poetry of it all.

BRYAN MORGAN, *The End of the Line*

All railways have what Lady Bracknell (in *The Importance of
Being Earnest*) called luggage trains. Even systems whose public
traffic is exclusively passenger, like the London Underground,
have 'luggage trains' used for carrying materials needed for
repairing the lines. Many railways, of course (in the U.S.A.,
the majority), carry nothing but freight. In any case, for most
systems freight forms the greater part of their business and so
it is perhaps a little odd that the only freight operation so far
mentioned is one carrying dishes round a rajah's dinner table.

On our own railways, passenger trains now predominate, but
this is due not to any incompetence or lack of enterprise on
the part of British railwaymen but rather to Britain's geography.
Rail freight transport is cheap because a large number of vehicles
can be joined together and hauled as one. But the collection
together of a train of vehicles all needing to go to the same
place is tedious and expensive; therefore if the distance to go
is short – as it inevitably is in a small island – trains become
less and less advantageous except for traffic like coal that in
any case moves around by the train-load. Which is what has

happened in Britain, where freight moves an average distance of only seventy miles from source to destination.

On a big continent where the average car of freight moves four times as far, things are different. For all that is wrong with the railroad systems of North America, a trip to observe the glorious pageant of freight movement there is certainly worth the modest fare now charged to cross the Atlantic. Certainly Britain has nothing (and Europe very little) to offer in comparison, although it is true that our liner trains convey containers that come from the ends of the earth. In recent years the number of owners of the cars which circulate on North American rails has diminished, but the hundreds that remain take advantage of a moving nationwide bill-board to blazon abroad their names. A mile-long freight can easily take five minutes or more to pass a level crossing – and what else is there for a waiting motorist to do but read the names and slogans on the cars? Even if only one in a million realized that Union Pacific, for example, was still in the transportation business and was able to offer his custom, it would be worthwhile. Other motorists grind their teeth with impatience, so making the few minutes' wait seem hours, but for such as us the names are the very stuff that railroad romance is made of . . . Rio Grande, Santa Fe, Canadian Pacific, Boston & Maine, Norfolk & Western, Katy, Burlington Northern, Union Pacific, Duluth, Missabe & Iron Range, Florida East Coast, Illinois Central Gulf and the rest.

It is really only in this indirect sort of way that most railway enthusiasts can get to know and enjoy the principal business of the world's railways. While he can experience personally their way with passengers by simply buying a ticket, it is more difficult for him to consign himself by freight train. One whole area of operation is therefore hidden from direct view. When forty years ago the R.A.F. used to go night after night to the Ruhr Valley to attack the marshalling yards at Hamm and elsewhere, people used to wonder what on earth 'marshalling' meant; that is, until it was explained that it was just a grand word for shunting.

Incidentally, the German railway installations proved very resilient to such attentions.

The shunting of loose vehicles – which is what marshalling yards are all about – is almost without exception totally prohibited when those vehicles carry human passengers. Oddly enough, one place where an exception is made is at one of the main entrance points to one of the most careful nations in the world, Basle in northern Switzerland. Trains arrive from Germany, Belgium, the French Channel ports and Paris, carrying through carriages for Austria, Italy via the St Gotthard Tunnel as well as Berne and beyond. In each case these carriages have to be dealt out on to the outgoing trains like a hand at cards. This is done by drawing the train out of the station and uncoupling what in marshalling yard parlance is called a cut of cars. A kick from the shunting engine sends the cut, complete with happy holidaymakers and in the charge of a blue-smocked shunter, free-wheeling into the appropriate platform.

What is fun for the participants in this case is less so for railwaymen when they are faced not with a hundred or so cars to sort daily for three or four destinations, but with thousands to sort for hundreds of destinations. That is an operation which the enthusiast can only see by special permission and in an organized group.

15. Permanent way at Bristol
East Junction.

16. Relaying the permanent way
at Picton, North Yorkshire, in
July 1959.

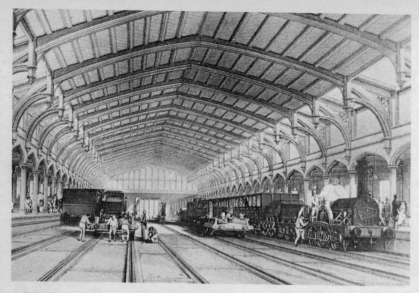

17. Brunel's superb train shed at Bristol, as completed in 1841.

18. A special steam train of the Rhaetian Railway crosses the beautiful Landwasser Viaduct near Filisur, Switzerland.

19. A first-class car of the 'Flying Scotsman' express following a derailment on the northern outskirts of Newcastle in 1926.

20. The southbound 'Coronation' Express of the London and North Eastern Railway climbs away from Newcastle-upon-Tyne in 1938.

21. Luxury in excelsis: dining on South African Railways' famous 'Blue Train'.

22. Cleanliness and simplicity: meal service for two Western tourist groups on the People's Railways of China.

23. A Darjeeling–Himalayan train negotiates the Batasia loop in November 1978.

24. Little trains: a preserved Great Western Railway auto-train runs on the Wallingford branch, Berkshire.

25. No. 45428 and owner.

26. The late Bishop Treacy leans from the cab of preserved 4–6–0 No. 5428 *Eric Treacy*.

27. No. 5428 *Eric Treacy* as restored to London, Midland & Scottish Railway livery.

28. Blue Peter re-naming ceremony at Doncaster Works, November 1970.

29. British Railways' last steam locomotive, 2–10–0 *Evening Star*, is the first one to be turned on the new turntable at Didcot, 17 August 1980. A well-known disc jockey performed the ceremony.

30. The one-time course of the Lynton & Barnstaple Railway at Barnstaple, Devon.

31. New trains: a 'Fairlie' type 0–4–0 locomotive, built in 1979, negotiates the new Deviation line, also completed in 1979, on the Ffestiniog Railway in North Wales.

16 · DINNER IN THE DINER

Dinner in the diner, nothing could be finer
Than to have your ham and eggs in Carolina.

GLENN MILLER, *Chattanooga Choo-Choo*

Railway refreshment-room food – often not at all bad – has been the subject of unkind jokes ever since Liverpool & Manchester days. On the other hand, its counterpart, the railway dining-car meal, induces a degree of reverence which, if you stop and think, is hardly deserved. Yet there is some magic that turns an indifferent repast in the diner into an acceptable one and one of modest quality into a memorable meal. Of course, there are some trains which offer food of a quality concerning which there is no dubiety. One such can be found (at the time of writing) any mid-day in Paris's Gare de Lyon, ready to serve you the kind of lunch that can just be squeezed in before Lyons in 2 hours 55 minutes time. But stay, here you are being tantalized because by the time this is set in print the 'Mistral' express will have been replaced by a Train Grande Vitesse, so fast there is not time for a proper meal and so no diner, and pre-cooked tray meals only at your seat. Never mind, there might be some canned Beaujolais at the bar, remembering as you pull the ring to open it that consumption of some famous wines is said to be more than double the amount produced. One thinks with nostalgia of times when that excellent French railway magazine *La Vie du Rail* could print such things as a cartoon of man in dining car examining menu and saying (in French) to the steward: 'Steamed potatoes? ... but I thought this line was electrified.' It does seem likely though that proper French *wagon-restaurant* meals will continue to be served in some expresses such as the 'Aquitaine' and 'L'Étendard' during their 360-mile 230-minute non-stop runs between Paris and Bordeaux; even an average speed of 94 mph does not preclude a proper meal.

Most French railway meals were until a few years ago served in the elegant blue or varnished teak dining cars of the legendary Compagnie Internationale des Wagons-Lits et des Grands Express Européens. Although 'Madame la Compagnie' still operates in the background, most of the restaurant cars now belong to the railway administrations. I am not quite certain whether the meals served were always quite up to their reputation, but both the original vehicles as well as traditional *haute cuisine* catering can be sampled in various 'nostalgia' excursion trains composed of the famous old vehicles. Intraflug Ltd is running the 'Nostalgic Orient Express' (Zurich–Istanbul), the 'Belle Époque Express' (Paris–Monte Carlo), the 'Aegean Express' (Zurich–Athens) and the 'Champagne Express' (Zurich–Rheims) in 1981; another organization has acquired some of the old cars to run via the cross-channel train ferries (on which the regular London–Paris sleeping cars have just ceased operating) from London to Venice. Details can be found in Thomas Cook's *Continental and Overseas Timetables*.

Everyone perhaps has one meal which stands out even in a lifetime's eating on trains. For this writer it was the climax of a journey to Switzerland in 1946 just after the war. The French railways had problems (which for once resulted in a dinner bad even for the time), accentuated by the need for walking-pace negotiation of several shooflys (diversions) round damaged bridges and creeping passages across numerous temporarily repaired ones. The 450 miles from Calais to Basle (where there was just time for a *café complet* at the buffet) took fourteen hours, but at about lunchtime we changed onto the narrow gauge at a place called Landquart. The Rhaetian Railway's connection to Davos and St Moritz via Filisur was waiting and there attached to it was one of their little crimson-lake and gold dining cars. Even now I remember that the dish of the day was Crêpes Valaisane, a confection of diced veal wrapped in pancakes, washed down by equally delicious Swiss Veltiner wine. The sun shone on the snow and seven years of rationing and austerity seemed suddenly somehow very far away as we climbed on up into the mountains. All of which perhaps explains why Swiss restaurant-car meals are here declared to be high up in any *Good Railway Food Guide*, and with them the German, whose excellent dining cars serve rather similar food at surprisingly modest prices. Incidentally, in summer those Rhaetian Railway dining cars make forays on to neighbour Furka-Oberalp, to provide sustenance on the 'Glacier Express' between St Moritz and Zermatt. The F-O is in part a cog railway with 1 in 9 gradients. Would the 'Glacier Express' have the world's steepest meals-on-wheels, then?

Eating on American trains has a special ring to it, because a time is still within the memory of people living now when by far the best food in the United States was served in railroad dining cars. That this is no 'giants of old' tale is borne out by what was available on the Atchison, Topeka & Santa Fe Railroad's 'De Luxe' express from Chicago to Los Angeles, which followed the 'California Limited' and preceded the 'Chief' and the 'Super Chief' as the flag train on the route. The bill of fare in 1911 contained the following items, all offered *à la carte*:

Oysters – Blue Points, fried, broiled or milk stew
Sardines   Caviar   Chow Chow   Olives
Bacon, broiled or fried   Ham, broiled or fried
Bacon and Eggs   Ham and Eggs

Eggs – boiled, fried, scrambled, poached-on-toast or shirred
Omelette – plain, ham, parsley, tomato, mushroom or rum

Steak, tenderloin or sirloin – with french peas, mushrooms, bacon,
bordelaise sauce or béarnaise sauce
Chicken – broiled or fried
Mutton chops – plain, with bacon or with tomato sauce
Cold Tongue   Cold Ham   Boston Baked Beans, hot or cold

Potatoes – french fried, au gratin, mashed, browned Lyonnaise
or julienne
Salad – lettuce, potato or chicken

Vienna bread   Tea Biscuit   Boston Brown Bread
Dry toast   Buttered toast   Milk toast
Shredded Wheat with Cream

Assorted Fruit   Preserved Strawberries   Preserved Figs
Orange Marmalade

Roquefort Cheese and Crackers

Coffee, Cocoa, Chocolate with whipped cream, milk
malted milk
Tea – Ceylon, Young Hyson, English Breakfast, Special Blend

Considering the complexity of this list, one now perhaps
understands the reason for that excellent U.S. custom of writing
out your own check or bill as you go. All the items were
individually priced, but one would similarly write out one's
order for chosen items on a *table d'hôte* menu. Even when, as
often in Canada, meals were included in the fare, the same
system applied. As passenger trains fell on hard times after the
Second World War, luxury meals began to disappear, although
a few trains maintained the old standards right up to Doomsday,
1 January 1970, the day when Uncle Sam's own passenger train
preservation operation, known to us as Amtrak, took over.
Illinois Central's 'Panama Limited' from Chicago to New
Orleans was one which kept up the old standards until the end.
Their 'King's Dinner' could consist of the following:

Manhattan or Martini Cocktail
(Swirler Service or On-the-Rocks)

Appetizers

French Gulf Shrimp Cocktail
or
Crab Fingers
(Special Sauce)

A 13-oz. bottle of imported Bertoli Vinrosa

The Fish Course

Charcoal Broiled Boneless Sirloin Steak
Buttered Mushroom Slices
Your choice of Potato and Vegetable
A special Salad (created by your Waiter)
Dinner Bread

A heady Cheese with fresh Apple Wedges
Toasted Saltines

I. C. Coffee

Crème de Cacao, Crème de Menthe or
Blackberry Liqueur

Amtrak, which inherited not only 117 dining cars but also many staff and much tradition from the railroad companies, used to offer a high standard of simple meals but now have resorted to airline-style catering.

The British dining car, without being in any way special, has always offered reasonable meals accompanied by surprisingly good wine, though only breakfast seems to reach gourmet standards. In spite of this (or maybe because of it) much of the world outside Europe and North America serves good solid English nursery food in its dining cars. Few people got tired of ten days of such meals served on the 'Sunset Limited' rail tour of South Africa, punctuated by occasional hiccups when the electrics of the vintage clerestory dining cars showed signs of temperament. Some enhancement and variation were produced by Afrikaaner specialities such as mealie-meal or sorghum porridge for breakfast, as well as steak or mince on toast to follow. South African Railways do a marvellous marmalade pudding, even if it is better suited to British weather than African!

British-style eating on trains suffered a fairly rich sea change when it was transplanted to India. The absence of corridors and the presence of large amounts of manpower favour a different system. At station A a man comes aboard to take orders for meals. He gets off at Station B and telegraphs forward the requirements to station C, where the meals are prepared. Other men bring them when the train stops. They are then eaten (a little colder than when they left the kitchen, like meals in an old-fashioned stately home) and the trays are then collected at station D, finally being taken back on the next train. Oh, yes, I nearly forgot, someone else gets on at station D to collect the money, thereby bringing station E into the picture as the place he gets off. One thing the system does have in common with the British is that, as regards Western world food, its breakfasts are its best.

Another railway system in whose restaurant cars can rather unexpectedly be found good (but strangely unfamiliar) wine is the Chinese. Provided one has learnt the knack of using chopsticks, what P. G. Wodehouse called 'the browsing and the sluicing' are excellent. Chinese-style dishes (but not very like the ones we are used to in Britain) keep coming along and the problem is only to conserve one's appetite for the later ones. Impeccable cleanliness and courteous service naturally go without saying. This discussion of the pleasures of eating on trains accordingly concludes with appreciation of a faraway railway whose meals are not only amongst the best but have also only recently been made available to us.

17 · READING AND THE BATH

Not only was the Great Western the best line with the fastest trains and the most powerful engines but it also had carriages reserved for 'Reading' and the 'Bath'.

ANON., quoted in *The Cheltenham Flyer* by
W. G. Chapman (*G.W.R. carriages were often
labelled for Reading and Bath*)

It is when night falls that even the most ardent train-lover sometimes begins to think there might be something in that ten-times speed advantage possessed by the great jets above. Dinner is over, nothing can be seen out of the windows, company in the bar is uncongenial, so what to do? Reading is part of the answer and, since there are at least 500 million words of English written on railways, no one can complain of lack of choice. Even reading the books written about railway books could take one across India, even if not perhaps across Siberia. Nearly every chapter in this has touched on the literature of that particular facet of the hobby discussed therein, and there is no aspect of the railway scene uncovered from dry-as-dust technical or legal treatises to frothy novels.

It would seem a good idea to fit the punishment to the crime. One might, when travelling in India for instance, take Kipling's *Kim* (and find rail travel surprisingly little changed), Professor Westwood's *Railways of India*, H. R. F. Keating's *Inspector Ghote Takes the Train*, and, of course, John Masters' *Bhowani Junction*. It always seemed to this writer until he went there that Masters had been drawing the long bow a trifle when he described how Victoria Jones took a shower in a train after riding with her father on the engine. Of course, anyone who has travelled in India will recognize the shower business as quite authentic, since they are a feature of the wash-places on even quite ordinary trains in India. Incidentally, the description of that ride on the engine seen through the eyes of a frightened girl is one of the best bits of railway narrative writing ever done.

While we are on the subject of 'the Bath', whether shower or otherwise, the old 'Twentieth Century Limited' offered between New York and Chicago not only ordinary baths but also salt-water ones. Should one ever cross America by this route, Lucius Beebe's evocative book on this most famous of all trains might well be a companion for any dark lonely hours there might be. If one expects to feel a little sad about the comforts and services now no longer available on today's slightly homespun 'Lake Shore Limited', successor to the 'Century', it would nicely compensate to take Robert Louis Stevenson's *Across the Plains* when proceeding on the next stage by 'San Francisco Zephyr'. He writes: '[the cars] destined for emigrants on the Union Pacific are only remarkable for their extreme plainness, nothing but wood entering in any part into their construction, and for the usual inefficacy of the lamps, which often go out and shed but a dying glimmer even while they burn. The benches are too short for anything but a young child.'

Beebe's *Overland Limited* could still tantalize you beyond Chicago and, of course, there is Zane Gray's *Down the Roaring UP Trail* for light relief. *Steam Across the Divide* by William Kratville, as well as that same author's *Big Boy*, would probably constitute an overdose of nostalgia.

One could at one time cross the Pacific by superb railway-owned steamers belonging to Canadian Pacific (*Canadian Pacific – An Illustrated History*, by C. Dorin) – and then have a tour of Japan under the guidance of Charles Small's *Rails to the Rising Sun*.

That master of the short story Somerset Maugham wrote a story (hardly at all about trains) called 'The Book Bag' which began by describing the large bag of reading matter without which he never travelled. One might well need a book bag to carry even a selection of the books on the next stage across Russia, starting with Maugham's own delightful *Mr Harrington's Washing* (from 'Ashenden'), augmented by Eric Newby's rather disrespectful *The Big Red Train Ride* and that excellent history of the Trans-Siberian *To the Great Ocean*, by Harmon Tupper (Secker & Warburg, 1965). Concerning railways in Poland, there seems to be a shortage of books – indeed the only one on your author's shelves is what is apparently an account, written in Polish, of a small-gauge railway near Warsaw. It is by Symeon Surgiewicz and is called *Chuchie* – a title which needs no translation – but is not a children's book, for the illustrations include one or two of the methods used by the conquering Germans during the war to discourage any patriotic action by the staff. Karl Maedel's *Unvergessene Dampflokomotive* could take one across the two Germanies, and the official 125th anniversary book of the Netherlands Railways (with enchanting illustrations even if you can't make out all the text) *Der Trein Hoort Erbis* for the next stage will do for Holland. But soon enough it will be time to open *British Railway Steamers* (published by Ian Allan), before Cecil J. Allen himself takes us up from Harwich on his own railway (he began his railway career as a Great Eastern man) occupied with his history of the line (also published by Ian Allan). In respect for the great man's memory we should perhaps prepare ourselves a timing list beginning:

miles			
0·0	Parkeston Quay	dep.	0·00
3·8	Wrabness		
7·7	Mistley		
10·4	MANNINGTREE		
12·9	Ardleigh		

... and so on over Brentwood Summit and down through Ilford, Stratford and Bethnal Green to that busiest of all termini, Liverpool Street Station, London.

Bracketing all these works of local interest are such globe-trotting railway books as Paul Theroux' *The Great Railway Bazaar* and *The Old Patagonian Express*, not to speak of Christopher Portway's *Corner Seat*. Helpful to the world traveller but on a lower plane than these is *Atlas of the World's Railways* (Bison Books, 1981). In fact, reference books for rail travellers are almost as old as railways. Osborne's *Guide to the Grand Junction Railway* was published as early as 1838, but this writer's choice (as you by now will expect) is the Great Western Railway's *Through the Window – Paddington to Penzance*, plus one or two of their never excelled 'Boys of All Ages' series such as *Locos of the Royal Road* or *The Cheltenham Flyer* (also reprinted, by Patrick Stephens Ltd).

But, you may say, all this is solid stuff; what about those frothy novels spoken of earlier? Easily top in frothiness comes *Love on a Branch Line* by John Hadfield, which tells of a crazy crippled peer with three beautiful daughters, who contentedly lives on a train (steam, of course), because his stately home has been requisitioned by the Civil Service and then forgotten about. The stately home's peacock plays a decisive role in the plot, and this reminds us of Winston Clewes' book *Peacocks on the Lawn* (Michael Joseph, 1952), an account of the people involved in, as well as the building, running and, finally the demise of a narrow-gauge railway in the West of Ireland. While the book is fiction, all the amazing accidents and incidents contained in the plot did actually happen there, but on different railways. So far from having to draw upon his imagination, the author needed to tone down the truth to give some credibility to the story!

John Snell's *Jennie* (Nelson, 1958), a little more sentimental in style, did a similar thing for narrow-gauge railways in Wales. It was a remarkable achievement for a boy of eighteen and his friends are still hoping for another, even after more than twenty years. His last chapter ends with the weeds growing amongst the remains; now, of course, we know that in real life there is a happier ending.

America's narrow-gauge railways are immortalized in Carl Fallberg's enchanting collection of cartoons called *Fiddletown & Copperopolis – The Line of Least Resistance*. The detail on the drawings – not for nothing was Carl Fallberg Walt Disney's Chief Animator – is such that they have to be *read*, not just looked at. They go from 'Distinguished Citizens of Fiddletown & Copperopolis Meet to Charter an Uncommon Carrier' via 'The Realization of a Great Dream – Driving the Golden Spike at Bicarbonate of Soda Springs' to 'Bum's Rush Given Eastern Junk Dealers Attempting to Buy F. & C. for Scrap'. There is not only an excellent map but also a working timetable; both show a station called 'Solitary Stump – Formerly Lone Pine'! Something rather similar – but this time for the broad not the narrow gauge – was produced by W. Heath Robinson in 1935 (and since reprinted) called *Railway Ribaldry*.

Less frothy is C. Hamilton-Ellis's *Dandy Hart*. This is a vigorous historical novel – like the Old Testament, full of blood and lust – about the life of a locomotive engineer, son of a coaching proprietor who was put out of business by the railways. The hero is involved in various well-known incidents, such as the Battle of Havant, where the London & South Western and the London Brighton & South Coast Companies' men actually came to blows over the latter's access to Portsmouth.

Currently there are eight monthly English-language periodicals devoted to the pleasures of railways. Each has its own slant, though one cannot help feeling there is an element of a game of musical chairs in the present situation. In spite of what Glen Miller sang, one magazine will by no means take you from New York to Baltimore, a 2¾-hour journey; but like good wine, good magazines improve with age and a ten-year-old (or more) bound volume is an excellent way of making the miles fly by. And so to bed.

18 · SLEEPING IN THE SLEEPER

In walked Gottschalk, gay, debonair,
intrepid Gottschalk of the Compagnie
Internationale des Wagons-Lits ...

J. B. MORTON ('BEACHCOMBER')
A Bonfire of Weeds

Train eating may give an uplift to the quality of the food, but train sleeping even at its best gives a sharp downlift to the quality of the sleep. In Britain this is specially the case at the moment, as the present B.R. sleeping-car fleet, which is very much all of an age, nears the end of its life of some twenty-five years. Let us hope that the new vehicles on order will do for train sleep what eating on the train does for food. Amongst the pleasures of railways is to think of the changes one would make oneself if one ran B.R., and this is a case in point. Why time the night trains from Glasgow to London, say, to do the journey in six and a half hours (which requires quite a lot of 90 mph running) when an eight-hour timing would mean slower and steadier running and when the trains anyway stand for one and a half hours and more at Euston after arriving there soon after 5 am? And when also the slower running would make the night passenger trains more compatible with liner (container) trains and the like?

I recall a trip down to Cornwall when those now ageing B.R. sleeping cars were new. A word to the attendant about the comfortable ride in this then modern car produced the response, 'It's not one of ours, sir,' implying of course that it was not

Great Western and therefore couldn't be any good. But there was something better than the carriage and this had *not* changed – traditional G.W.R. courtesy, proof against even the most tiresome of clients. Perhaps you know the old story about the man who found he had company in his G.W.R. sleeper. He received a charming and disarming reply from Paddington, spoilt just a little by the fact that by mistake they had enclosed his original letter of complaint endorsed, 'Send the bug letter'.

Railways in Britain, as well as those built and run under British influence, traditionally ran their own sleeping cars and this arrangement on the whole continues. In Southern Africa custom has moved far enough away from those of the original British for there to be a compulsory 6 am cup of *coffee* (not tea!) served in the sleeping compartments. In India the British sleeping car has evolved into something rather basic; I remember a group *en route* from Agra to Lucknow which was largely composed of first-time visitors to that crowded land and who had a vision of crisp sheets waiting for them after a hot day's sightseeing; and their viewing with horror the dusty and primitive interior of their first-class Indian sleeping car. I also remember them two train nights later (confidently) setting to and making the very basic amenities of our 'bogie' into something comfortable.

The continental European sleeper car was a legend; just as they did with their diners, the Compagnie Internationale des Wagons-Lits provided really satisfactory comforts for the long-distance traveller. The layouts of the cars were little different from the British, with transverse berths in small compartments, although for equivalent accommodation and an equivalent overnight journey the supplement would be three or four times greater. 'Wagons-Lits' did, however, have a certain style, which somehow B.R. and its predecessors never quite achieved. It may be that the tables are turning now that the individual railways of Europe are taking over the Wagons-Lits cars. The literature as well as the cinema of the Wagons-Lits is extensive, reflecting the fascination of a company who could take you from London to Baghdad (except for a ferry trip at Istanbul) and whose services have covered, at one time or another, railways the whole way from Lisbon to Shanghai. The cars never actually covered quite the whole distance from Oslo to Aswan on the River Nile; apart from the Istanbul ferry there was a bus sector in Palestine and a boat ride across the Suez Canal, even in those rare years when all was well politically elsewhere.

Amongst the pleasures of journeying by Wagons-Lits can be included playing with all the delightful gadgets, turning on and off the combinations of room lights, reading lights and blue night-lights, and wishing perhaps that one had a gold repeater to hang on the hook of the little padded watch-holder. Also there was the nice thought that the conductor would see to all the customs men, immigration officials, ticket collectors and security police who would pester less fortunate travellers during the night. These magnificent men in their smart brown uniforms were very much a symbol of safety and security; so much so that people like your author had no qualms about entrusting young sons and daughters to them for long journeys across the frontiers of Europe, in spite of the deep and quite unconscious conviction common to so many Brits that the jungle begins at Calais.

Wagons-Lits had no use for anything but their full title, which was displayed in various languages in gold leaf on the outside of their magnificent blue vehicles – or in brass letters on the older teak ones. On one side, French was almost always used; on the other the language was that of the country to which the car was allocated or which its clients would be most likely to understand. The only use of English for the company's title was on some new steel cars supplied for services in China during 1925, but others were more common, for example:

COMPAGNIE INTERNATIONALE DES WAGONS-LITS
ET DES GRANDS EXPRESS EUROPEENS

INTERNATIONAL EISENBAHN SCHLAFWAGEN GESELLSCHAFT

COMPAGNIA INTERNAZIONALE DELLE CARROZZE CON LETTI
E DEI GRANDI TRENI ESPRESSI EUROPEI

COMPANHIA INTERNACIONAL DAS CARRUAGENS-CAMAS
E DOS GRANDES EXPRESSOS EUROPEOS

AYRUPA SÜRAT KATALARI VE BEYNELMILEL YATAKLI
VAGONLAR SIRKETI

KANSAINUALINEN MAKUUVANU — JA EUROOPAN
PIKAJUNAYHTIO

ΔΙΕθΝΗΣ ΕΤΑΙΡΙΑ ΤΩΝ ΚΛΙΝΑΜΑΞΩΝ ΚΑΙ ΤΩΝ ΤΑΧΕΙΩΝ
ΕΓΡΩΠΑΙΚΩΝ ΑΜΑΞΟΣΤΟΙΧΙΩΝ

The use of Greek is a reminder of one pleasure denied the patrons of the company. In Serbia, where the line ran along the River Vardar on the route from Belgrade to Athens, conductors had instructions on warm days to pull down the blinds to preserve the modesty of young local girls bathing *puris naturalibus* in the stream.

Another version of this story, not only more romantic but also a little more credible, is that a traveller (described as 'an Englishman') had seen a beautiful naked girl bathing in the Vardar, got out at the next station, found her and then married her. The consequence was that many of the young ladies of the area took to timing their baths to suit the running of the Orient Express and the company felt their customers needed protection.

Talking of bathing, Wagons-Lits bath cars were almost unknown, although there were showers in the baggage cars of both the Simplon-Orient and Rome expresses. A notable exception was the fitting of a bath compartment in one de luxe car (type LX) of the Blue Train (more correctly the 'Côte d'Azur Express') specially for the use of H.R.H. the Prince of Wales, later (and briefly) King Edward VIII, when he travelled for a holiday in the South of France.

Pullman of America also had a legendary reputation, attention to every detail making it a well-deserved one. At its peak Pullman offered over 100,000 beds every night on a fleet of over 10,000 cars. But there was one fundamental difference between the European sleeping car and the American – in the latter the berths were longitudinal and not transverse. The reason for this difference was that each type of sleeping car grew out of the respective ordinary day coach. In Europe the transverse seats in the compartment coach are natural beds and the sleeping compartment with transverse berths evolved from them. In America the normal carriage had a centre aisle and seats on either side, much too short to serve as beds; so the berths had to be longitudinal. In both cases space was saved by making two stories (occasionally three) with upper and lower berths. The lower berth was obviously preferable and in North America this was recognized by charging a higher price. I think also that one sleeps better longitudinally in a train than transversely.

Originally privacy was obtained by drawing dark-green curtains either side of the central aisle, but after 1937 came the 'roomette', which had little cabins either side of what had now become a central passageway. Later came 'drawing rooms', which was the name for compartments in the European style, in many of which the beds were set transversely.

George Mortimer Pullman began revolutionizing travel in the U.S.A. (and eating his competitors) in 1859, almost ten years before George Nagelmackers, who founded Wagons-Lits, started doing the same for Europe. Britain, betwixt and between as always, opted first to go the Pullman way, with sleeping-car services operated by Pullman from London's St Pancras Station to Scotland and elsewhere. In the end the railways in Britain built and ran their own, and the Pullman Car Company's British subsidiary was taken over by native interests in which a man called Davidson Dalziel (later Lord Dalziel) played a leading role. British Pullman then specialized in providing what in America were called 'parlour cars', and the name entered the language over here as well, but with a different meaning, symbolizing comfortable armchairs, shaded table lights, thick carpets and good food, whereas in America the meaning tends towards horizontal rather than vertical comfort, although Pullman parlour and dining cars were common.

Finally, there is always the question of what to do when all the sleeping berths are taken. One solution is related by Charles Small in *Rails to the Rising Sun*. He suggests a drink called a 'lower berth': two bottles of saké combined with a treble whisky made it possible to pass out for the night even in a seat designed for the small stature of the Japanese. He does admit, though, that the problem of the morning after was not wholly solved.

19 · AT THE JUNCTION

She caught the train she said she would,
She changed at junctions as she should.

ROSE HENNIKER HEATON, 'The Perfect Guest'
(from *The Perfect Hostess*)

There is such a thing as a painless railway junction. I mean by that the sort with no station platforms in sight, where a great main line divides into two nearly as great. Wootton Bassett Junction west of Swindon is one example, Heaton Lodge Junction near Huddersfield is another, Grand Junction near Birmingham is a third. Shaftholme Junction, that famous ploughed field north of Doncaster where the Great Northern Railway ended, is a fourth. No point in looking them up in timetables, but now that even their signal boxes have gone, a rail-fan can take pleasure in the secret knowledge of their identity and passage.

Still to be found in the timetables is the greatest junction in the world, though it is still effectively a painless one. This is Clapham Junction, which has seventeen long platform lines and a train every fifteen seconds or so either passing through or stopping. It could be said though that the sight of this tremendous flow of traffic on all these parallel lines (Clapham is not even a junction in the sense that the various lines merge there) is certainly one of the railway wonders of the world. One could add that the sight of the action there is also one of the world's top railway pleasures. Over 2,000 trains pass each weekday.

This brings us to the least busy junction in the world. Croesor Junction, near Porthmadog, North Wales, on the old Welsh Highland Railway, must have been served by fewer trains in its whole existence of thirteen years than Clapham sees in a few days.

But none of the junctions so far mentioned is one of the ordinary kind, the sort that you change trains at when making a journey that needs more than one train. For railway enthusiasts, the very great pleasure that they find in ordinary railway junctions, because of all the activity that goes on there, is especially enhanced by their being absolute hell for non-enthusiasts. 'If people *must* be married why *must* they be married in the *bowels* of the country on a hot day, a complete slug of a train and two *diabolical* changes. You know, my dear, all that climbing over bridges for platform four ...,' wrote A. P. Herbert in *The Trials of Topsy*. It is startlingly appropriate that (on earth) Hell is the name of an important, and no doubt well-named, railway junction (and little else) in Norway. Junctions everywhere are only too liable to have connections so tight that trains are missed, or so lax that there are boring hours to kill. Cheerless refreshment rooms, vandalized waiting rooms, shut bookstalls, draughty platforms, as well as many other inconveniences and annoyances often combine to add to the miseries of changing trains.

The old companies used to recognize this; let us go back fifty years and see how passengers were spared the unholy ritual of changing trains on their way to the West Country by two deservedly famous trains. A profusion of 'through' and 'slip' coaches were carried, as shown in the table on the next page.

The 'slip' coaches were dropped at the junctions named without the main train stopping. Slipping was a fascinating facet of operation which is now history. Each 'slip' had its 'slip guard' on duty at the leading end of each specially equipped slip coach. There were special slipping distant signals at places where slips were dropped; on receiving the 'all clear' the slip guard would

Cornish Riviera Express		*Atlantic Coast Express*	
10.30 from Paddington		11.00 from Waterloo	
to Penzance		to Ilfracombe	
THROUGH COACHES		THROUGH COACHES	
Junction	*Destination*	*Junction*	*Destination*
		Templecombe	Local stations to Exeter
Westbury (slip)	Weymouth	Sidmouth Junc.	Sidmouth
Taunton (slip)	Minehead	Exeter	Exmouth
Taunton (slip)	Ilfracombe	Exeter	Padstow
Exeter (slip)	Kingsbridge	Barnstaple	Torrington
Par	Newquay	Halwill Junc.	Bude
Truro	Falmouth	Okehampton	Plymouth via Tavistock
St Erth	St Ives		

pull the slipping lever and his carriage would part from the main train. Careful control of the brake was necessary to bring the 'slip' to a stand at the platform. Unlike most trains, one that slips coaches is *permitted* to become divided and, because the tail-lamp carried by a train is a tell-tale that the train is intact, special double and triple tail-lamps were carried by trains which contained slip portions, as follows:

At rear of main train: two lamps, red above red
At rear of first slip portion: two lamps, red alongside white
At rear of second slip portion: two lamps, red above white
At rear of third slip portion: three lamps arranged in triangle, two red, one white

The Cornish Riviera Express would thus leave Paddington with nine lighted tail-lamps. If you add the two side-lamps at one time carried by each slip portion, as well as the headlights on the engine, that makes seventeen oil-lamps in all. And someone had to fill, trim and light them, as well as bring them to the train.

Slipping was prohibited in fog and falling snow and this give rise to the famous story of an Up West of England express making an unbooked call at Reading to detach a slip coach. Professor Joad of the Brains Trust once told how he was waiting for a London train and started to board this one. A porter shouted, 'Sir, this train doesn't stop here,' and (as the train started to move) Joad replied with perfect logic, 'Well, in that case I'm not getting on.'

To show what changes have been found necessary in the name of progress, twenty-five years later travellers to all the places served by these trains except Padstow, Weymouth and Plymouth had to change trains except on certain peak summer Saturdays. Small wonder that of the others only Newquay, Falmouth and Exmouth have trains at all today. The only counterparts to these fascinating complexes in the present-day world of railways are the through carriages run on the international trains of continental Europe. Even though in most cases these combine a variety of starting points with a variety of destination, as many as eight different on one train at the same time cannot be matched.

All the same, foreign junctions have not quite the same air about them, mainly I think because the raised platforms normal in Britain are not there to delineate the various routes. Take, for example, Sargans on the Swiss Federal Railways, the famous junction in eastern Switzerland where you (often) change to go to Austria. The lines and platforms almost seem to merge, especially after a glass or two of nice Sarganser wine in the buffet – a case not of *vin du pays* but *vin du gare*! This is so sometimes even at six in the morning, when people engaged on clearing snow from the lines come in for a tumblerful before starting work. It could be said that Swiss junctions are less hellish for non-enthusiast passengers than anywhere else. For one thing, practically all Swiss stations are open, like any public place such as the town square; in fact there is usually no fence or wall to separate the street from the platform. It is sometimes just a little disconcerting at a station on a double track when your train comes in on the far one and you have to board it standing on the near one. For another thing, the running of the trains is both frequent and reliable, so that long waits are the exception, not the rule.

Amongst these so-called ordinary railway junctions are many whose arrangement and layout has a special appeal to the connoisseur of such things. In this writer's view the perfect railway junction should have three attributes. The first is that there should be nothing about it to distract from the trains, like (for example) a road leading to it. The second is that it should have platforms for each line it serves arranged in a vee. The third is that it should still be there and used. You might find it hard to believe that such a paragon exists, but Dovey Junction near Aberdovey in Wales is such a place, and a romantic one indeed it is, set in the marshes of the River Dovey estuary with distant mountains for a backcloth. Although steam locomotives (indeed, few locomotives of any kind) are no longer to be seen there, the diesel trains on the scenic routes which lead to and from this unsullied temple of the rails have proportionately more observation cars than any luxury streamliner that ever crossed the North American Rockies. Even at the age of fifteen, when this writer bought his first ticket to Dovey Junction, he realized that a ticket which was to take him to a station with no exit except by rail was likely to be symbolic of the rest of his life.

Dovey Junction has no known rival in this scale of junction perfection. The only possibility of going higher would be to find a triangular station with the same features. At one time there were four treasured triangular stations in Britain. One, familiar to most, was on the old Midland Railway at Ambergate, some fifteen miles north of Derby. It was very tidy and symmetrical, the platforms inside the triangle joining up near their ends. The second at Bishop Auckland in County Durham, was rather a jumble but still a complete triangle even if a rather lopsided one. The third was near Glasgow, at Rutherglen on the Caledonian Railway; but train services stopping at the least

used of its original sides were very much more long lost than
the others. The last was a remote outpost of the Great Northern
Railway, at the centre of a three-pointed star whence rails
radiated to Keighley, Halifax and Bradford respectively. This
was Queensbury in the West Riding; fewer dwellings even than
at Dovey Junction were visible from its platforms but, alas, a
cart road of a sort did lead to it, thereby calling the purity of
its junction-ness into question. Also, of course, none of the
triangular stations still exist as such.

Having ranged England, Scotland and Wales for interesting
junctions and also taken a glance outside the British Isles, you
may be wondering whether Ireland might not have anything to
offer. The answer is a very strong 'yes', with an Irish junction
whose peculiarities one finds hard to believe, even having seen
them first hand, and which by any reasonable standards of
measurement comes at the top of the railway-lover's scale of
delight. Limerick Junction (nowhere near Limerick!), on the
Dublin–Cork main line, was laid out as if to demonstrate, using
the hardest of hardware, that the Irish way of doing things was
their own. No purely verbal description can do this four-way
junction justice, so a diagram is provided (see next page).

The main principle is that all trains should come in backwards.
Dublin–Cork trains coming past A would halt at B and (after
points had been changed) reverse into the Dublin–Cork platform, the northern half of the main platform. Similarly Cork–
Dublin trains would pass C and reverse at D. Trains from
Waterford to Limerick come past E, rattled over the main lines,
reversed at F and set back into the Limerick platform. Those
from Limerick to Waterford had the most fun. They come past
F, take the line G via the back of the station, reverse at H and
set back into the Waterford platform. When leaving, they draw
out on to the spur H, set back round the back (G to F) and then
proceed.

Strangely enough the arrangement was quite a convenient
one for passengers because there were no footbridges to cross

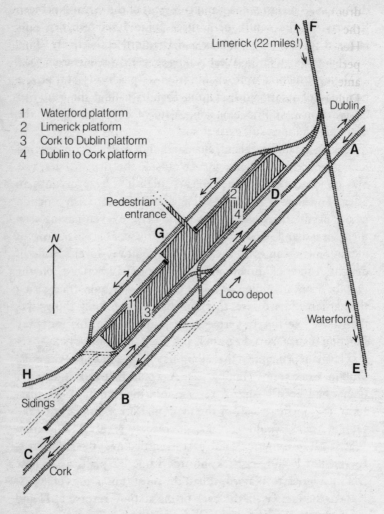

1 Waterford platform
2 Limerick platform
3 Cork to Dublin platform
4 Dublin to Cork platform

Limerick (22 miles!)

Dublin

Pedestrian entrance

N

Loco depot

Waterford

Sidings

Cork

Limerick Junction before 1967 (main running lines only)

when changing trains. It goes without saying that railway-lovers drool over the thought of the layout's absurdities and no doubt the staff accepted them because they made life interesting. Hence, benefits all round in a wholly Irish style. It should perhaps be added that the craziness of the layout was slightly ameliorated in 1967 when cross-overs were laid, allowing Dublin–Cork and Cork–Dublin trains to come alongside their respective platforms without reversing.

20 · LITTLE TRAINS

No one contemplating the pigs which now inhabit the bay platform at Gupworthy could imagine how passengers were to be garnered in these moorland wastes.

R. W. KIDNER, *English Light Railways*

Junctions are places where people change from big trains into lesser ones. You could also say that they are a change from one area of railway pleasure into another of equal or, to many, even greater stature.

When railway lovers count their blessings, high up on the list should come a series of booklets on the little railways of the British Isles. The author was R. W. Kidner, and the idea was so original that he had to found his own Oakwood Press (still flourishing) in the 1930s in order to publish them. More than anything else, these delightful pamphlets showed us that there was more to the pleasures of railways than mighty locomotives, famous expresses, huge stations and straight lines of metals leading over far horizons. Kidner drew our attention to railways that were almost too quaint to compete with the donkey but which always waited for Mrs Jones to finish her shopping on market days. His seven original literary efforts included a marvellously succinct description of each of about a dozen small railways. Since then most of the seventy-eight lines described have been the subject of individual full-size books – some of them have had several – many of which even now still come to us by virtue of the same Oakwood Press.

To pick a few flowers at random from a vast field ... The Culm Valley Railway ran from Tiverton Junction in Devon up the wide gently sloping Culm Valley to Hemyock. Why then did it twist and turn as if demented? The answer was that the land on which the line was built was given free on condition that it was constructed along the hedges of the fields. After it was taken over by the Great Western Railway (at a price which was the best that could be expected for a seller who had to sell and a buyer who did not want to buy) there was always difficulty in finding rolling stock that could go round the sharp curves.

The West Somerset Mineral Railway had no authority to carry fare-paying passengers – but it could let them ride free and charge for their shopping baskets over the twelve-mile ride from Watchet to Cupworthy. At Parracombe, on the Lynton & Barnstaple line not far away, one bought tickets at the village post office. Towards the other end of Somerset ran the quaint Weston, Clevedon & Portishead Railway – the line with the irresistible initials. Another line which is better written down in full is the enchanting though modernized little railway – even international in this case – called the Ferrovie e Autolinee Regionali Ticinesi which runs from Domodossola in Italy to Locarno in Switzerland, ending up running through the streets of the latter town.

The names of the stations were delightful too, and poetic rather than rude: for example, the Golden Valley Railroad ran from Pontrilas in Herefordshire to Hay-on-Wye in Wales via Abbeydore, Bacton, Vowchurch, Peterchurch, Dorstone and Westbrook. The north-east of England offered the more severe journey from Yarm to Battersby via Picton, Potto, Sexhow, Stokesly and Ingleby, while in Romansch Switzerland, *en route* from St Moritz to Zermatt, one passed successively through Versam-Safien, Valendas-Sagogn, Castrisch, Ilanz, Schnaus-Strada, Rueun, Waltensburg-Vuorz, Tavanasa-Breil, Trun, Rabius-Surrhein and Somvix-Compadials.

Of the Germanic little railways, those in Switzerland are

efficient and thus works of art of a kind slightly different from those which have pride of place here. It is in Austria that the personal element best intrudes; where else in the world would railways try to help themselves to survive by offering self-drive hire of steam locomotives, as is done on both the Zillertal Railway at Jenbach near Innsbruck and on the Murtal Railway at Murau in Southern Austria?

One basic oddity of the Austrian local railways was that the gauge was not the metric one of 750 mm but the slightly different English 2 feet 6 inches. The reason was that they derived from military railways and the original equipment was bought second-hand from an English contractor who had worked on the Suez Canal. There was nothing mean or slipshod, however, regarding the way the little railways of Austria were constructed. They remain an example to the world of a transport system that almost never obtrudes on a beautiful countryside. Even where it had to obtrude, as at stations, bridges and viaducts, the builders worked in such a way as to enhance rather than detract from pleasant villages and lovely scenery.

Solid construction was not a feature of all little railways. The Shropshire and Montgomeryshire Railway was originally intended to connect the Pottery district round Stoke-on-Trent with North Wales, but only the section running north-west out of Shrewsbury to nowhere in particular got built. The S. & M. (often spoken of as 'The Potts') had a viaduct at a place called Melverley which was in poor repair. Any reasonable railway would have just repaired it, but the 'Potts' – no follower – just bought lighter rolling stock, finally ending up with a horse tramcar and a tiny ancient three-ton steam locomotive called *Gazelle*. She was originally built in 1893 as personal transport for a certain William Burkett, an East Anglian railway magnate, who ran her regularly on lines around King's Lynn. *Gazelle* was light enough to give almost no anxiety in crossing the by now extremely fragile structure. Eventually during the Second

World War the military had need of railways that ran to nowhere and Melverley Viaduct got repaired.

France once had an enormous network of independent little railways, very few of which survive. In fact they began at Calais, at the town station, and the service offered, instead of being frequent, was exactly tailored to local needs, taking into account such matters as market days, saints' days and school holidays. Railway lovers of maturer years still drool over the eccentricities, but other users were less enthusiastic. Listen to Dornford Yates in *The Stolen March* (Ward Lock, 1932): '[In order to] demonstrate that the mind of a fool who built a drain which disappeared six hundred years ago was affected by the memory of the wall he pulled down to save himself the trouble of carting some new bricks ... I had to visit these towns. The first was sixteen miles distant. I went by train ... It took me three hours to go and nearly four to come back. I had forty minutes there and the station was a mile from the town ... [So] I had missed my breakfast, spent seven hours in torment and run two miles in the burden and heat of the day in order to purchase and consume two bottles of beer of a brand which compared unfavourably with that of Poitiers.'

I suspect that similar comments from non-railway enthusiasts applied in Spain, which was also once very rich in independent lines; now those few that remain have been both dieselized and nationalized. In the United States there are still a great many of what are called over there 'short lines', but quaintness is not usually now one of their characteristics. Elsewhere in the world much national independence seems to preclude local railway independence and so branch railways tend to be part of the main-line administrations. Even so, many top-class little trains meander out into the countryside under the banner of some great administration. The arrangement suited very well: locomotives, carriages, track could be hand-me-downs, while there was back-up in all sorts of forms to cope with any serious problems that arose; often the branch lines had some weight restriction and so heavier modern types could not be used. Your author used to work under the late Harold Robinson, who was Permanent Way Engineer at Wolverhampton and also a loco-motive enthusiast. He prolonged the life of the last Great Western '2021' class 0–6–0T for many years by refusing on entirely specious grounds to allow any other type down the Vinegar Branch at Worcester. This delightful railway connected Worcester Station with Lee & Perrins Worcester Sauce factory. It crossed two streets by ungated crossings at which standard railway semaphore signals were provided to control *road* traffic. The firm were very proud of the line; on one occasion in a letter written by someone new in the office it was referred to as 'your private siding'. They wrote in a furious reply that it was a proper railway incorporated by Act of Parliament and it existed long before the Great Western Railway got to Worcester!

The world title for quaintness and charm in this owned-by-big-brother class was (as one might expect) held by an Irish line. The Great Northern Railway of Ireland had a short branch from Fintona Junction to Fintona. Its little train used to be formed of a tram with first and second class inside and third class on top, while motive power was of the genuine hay-burning kind. The only trouble was that the horse was frightened of trains so it had to be kept out of sight of them until the junction was quiet. But, like nearly all the amazing little railways of Ireland, not only the Fintona branch but also the line which connected to it at the junction are just memories.

Exploring by train was (indeed, is) one of the greatest pleasures of railways, and while the scope in Britain, say, is less than it was, ease of access to the rest of the world more than compensates. It says enough that the fares on the famous 'Canopus' class flying boats of Imperial Airways between England and South Africa, India, China and Australia in the 1930s were very similar, measured in £s, to the excursion fares on jumbo jets today; whereas railway fares (say between London and Porthmadog for the Festiniog Railway) have increased by some twenty times.

The spacious land of India has some of the world's best little trains, measured of course on the rail-fan's scale and not that of serious users. For example, Siliguri in the plains of India may not be one of the nicest places in the world, but Darjeeling, 8,000 feet higher and distant a mere thirty-one miles as the crow flies, certainly is. Happily they are still connected by sixty miles of the greatest of great little railways of the world, even though the train takes seven hours or more and competing buses a mere four. As is well known, the alignment avoids big-time engineering by dodging obstacles with curves whose radii are as sharp as 66 feet and problems in the villages by running through the streets. There are four open-air spirals and five Z-reverses, but even so the grades are such that the famous little tank locomotives can haul only four tiny coaches, which means that the 'Mail' has to run in several parts, normally three. Since each locomotive carries a crew of five (driver, fireman, coal-passer and two brake- or sand-men) it could be said that the 'Darj' does its bit to cope with the problem of finding employment for India's teeming millions.

━━━━━━

We 'own' British Railways, but we are
allowed no say in them. We really do
own the Talyllyn Railway.

JOHN BETJEMAN,
Foreword to *Railway Adventure*

Until now we have thought only of pleasures that come by
chance from railways built for serious reasons – if you like,
railways which are unwitting instruments of pleasure. Plenty
of railways have been built solely and deliberately to give
pleasure – the first of them as early as 1808, when Richard
Trevithick, the Cornishman to whom the world's first full-size
steam locomotive is attributed, set up a circular track quite near
where Euston Station now stands and offered rides to a not
very enthusiastic populace. So you could say that steam passenger railways for pleasure preceded those for real, although
they have not become an epidemic until recent years.

A minor sort of epidemic resulted in the rash of railways
built to take the tourists of Queen Victoria's day to enjoy the
views from noted beauty spots. Naturally they were expected
to delight in the journey, but there was no question of any
intrinsic pleasure to be taken in the train itself. Perhaps it was
partly because the nineteenth-century railway mania left so few
other places for the railway engineer to go that there was this
late-Victorian rush to construct sight-seeing railways in the most
impossible places amongst the mountains. Now many fairly
normal railways run through the mountains and with these we
are not here concerned. Neither do we count as a railway any-

thing that is supported wholly by a cable – it must have rails, or certainly a rail.

The clientèle of these specialized railways for mountain climbing are almost always bent on pleasure. People go up in them for the views or perhaps to ski down, but at the same time they are full of interest for the railway-lover.

The home of the mountain railway is certainly Switzerland, whose engineers have contributed most of the technology and where most of the hardware can today be found. Yet passenger cog railways, which form the most important group of mountain railways, began in the U.S.A. when a man called Sylvester March obtained a charter for such a then unheard-of type of railway to the 6,293-foot summit of Mount Washington. During the debate in the New Hampshire legislature, an amendment was sarcastically proposed that the line should be continued to the moon. The railway was opened on 3 July 1869 but it has not led to any serious attempt to bring the majority of America's mountain peaks within the orbit of the iron road. Pikes Peak in Colorado is the only other contender, and after a period of exclusively diesel operation on its cog railway it is nice to hear that their surviving steam locomotive is being refurbished for tourist use. The Mount Washington Railroad is still 100 per cent steam in this its 111th year.

All the current records for steepness and length in the cog railway world are held by the Swiss. The prize which appeals is the one for steepness, and this the Pilatus Railway has held ever since it opened in 1879. The line rises 5,344 feet, from Alpnachstad to the upper station, close to the 6,800-foot summit of the mountain; the maximum gradient is 480 per 1,000 or about 1 in 2. Since there is a danger that a vertical cog-wheel might jump out of mesh on such a grade, the Pilatus line has a special horizontal double cog-wheel system known as the Locher after its inventor. 'Normal' cog railways have either the Riggenbach rack (which looks like a ladder) or the Abt (which on the ground looks like a double row of gear teeth). Points and crossings are possible with the Riggenbach and Abt systems, but impossible with the Locher. But here I seem to be beginning to indulge in a railway pleasure that is not always a pleasure to others – a delight in the nuts-and-bolts that sometimes runs away with the tongue or, as in this case, the pen.

Funiculars or cable-worked railways for both passengers and minerals, with which the world has been well stocked since before the days of steam, can go steeper even than Pilatus. Since a lift is really a cable-worked railway in which the rails are only used for guidance and not support, the idea of any record for steepness is not meaningful.

The longest and certainly the most complex totally cog-propelled railway in Switzerland, and therefore the world, is the enchanting twelve-mile Wengernalp-bahn in the Bernese Oberland. The faithful W.A.B. has been grinding up to the Kleine Scheidegg – the 'Clapham Junction of the Alps' it has been called – from both Wengen and Grindelwald since 1893. The separate locomotives and the wooden compartment cars, whose ticket collectors moved from compartment to compartment outside via the footboards, clinging on as best they could, have almost disappeared. Steam is even longer gone, for its reign ended seventy-two years ago, when the fleet of sixteen was withdrawn from service. A very good café beside the line just above Wengen (still there and still very good) was a useful place for a little refreshment. It is said that in steam days drivers used to let their engines go a little down the 1 in $5\frac{1}{4}$ gradient, by over-riding the automatic brake, in order to make up enough time for a quick one! Possibly this was safer than it sounds, for the new electric railcars come down at 10 mph, while steam was limited to $5\frac{1}{2}$. Swiss sloping-boiler steam rack locomotives still operate our own Snowdon Railway and operate on the Brienzer Rothorn Bahn, a neighbour of the W.A.B. Occasionally on a few other lines, including Pilatus, a long-set-aside steam locomotive is brought out.

Of forty-six cog-wheel pleasure lines listed in Walter Hefti's monumental *Zahnradbahnen der Welt* (Birkhauser Verlag, 1971), twenty outside Switzerland have closed. Even in that arch-non-closer-of-railways country, two have gone.

There are of course many more railway lines with rack *sections*, most of them normal commercial railways – ones that just need some help to get over some big hill or other. In some cases it is a very big hill indeed, as witness the original Trans-Andean railway from Mendoza in Argentina to Los Andes on the way to Valparaiso in Chile. Twenty-five miles of special triple Abt rack on a maximum gradient of 1 in $12\frac{1}{2}$ takes one over the 10,233-foot summit at La Cumbre.

Putting know-alls in their place is quite a railway pleasure and someone who might know the answer to the question 'which is the shortest U.S.A. railway route from the Atlantic to the Pacific?' might be floored by 'which railroad in the world hauls the heaviest loads?' The answer to both lies in the Panama Canal Zone, where the Panama Railroad crosses from ocean to ocean in a mere forty-eight miles and the Canal administration's cog-wheel 'mule' locomotives on the tow-paths move great ships in and out of the famous locks on a far from negligible eleven miles of rack railways, using Riggenbach rack of a special heavy pattern.

Of course there were normal railways as well as cog-wheel ones built to carry tourists to beauty spots, such as the long-closed one from Brighton to the Devil's Dyke on the downs above. But nowadays the term pleasure railway is usually reserved for lines on which the trains themselves form the attraction. One can cite examples where scenery is fairly minimal, such as the justly world-famous 15-inch gauge Romney, Hythe & Dymchurch Railway in Kent, whose miniature express trains running on a double-track main line comprise a monumental 'fix' of railway pleasure. But even where there are no suburban back gardens in the foreground, the flat scenery of Romney March is not really a consideration for the R.H. & D.R.'s 300,000 passengers carried each year. Kent is called the Garden of

England, but one of the two other pleasure railways there actually runs inside a paper works: the Sittingbourne & Kemsley is a delightful operation but the scenery is definitely negative! The remaining Kentish pleasure line is more the kind that one might expect, being a resuscitated light railway in pleasant country, known as the Kent & East Sussex Railway.

The K. & E.S.R. was typical of the little trains described in the last chapter, most of which have vanished – if they found it hard to compete against the donkey what chance had they against the motor bus? Most of those that survive do so purely because they have changed from arteries of commerce to instruments of pleasure. *Steam for Pleasure* (Routledge & Kegan Paul, 1976) is a worldwide survey covering 208 such lines. As regards those in Britain it would certainly not be possible to 'do' more than a fraction of them in one fortnight's holiday. You would need to spend several very pleasurable years' holidays to cover them reasonably comprehensively. Of course, the pleasures would not end there: before setting off there is the very real one of planning the whole expedition and after return there are the diaries, films and slides to savour, edit and catalogue.

But this is not the way to get the most out of living in the country which leads the world in the field of pleasure railways. Involvement will enhance enjoyment and will also give understanding of what it takes to run a railway. The scope is very wide. It begins with major operations like, shall we say, the Severn Valley Railway near Bridgnorth in Shropshire, which has over forty locomotives, sixty carriages and 10,000 members from which to draw volunteers. For a typical weekend's operations over a hundred volunteers will turn up to work on assignments as varied as can be imagined. Driving, firing, guard-ing, signalling, repairing, painting, cleaning, selling and cooking are just a few.

At the other end of the scale is the little railway which brings visitors from the car park some half a mile to Fort Benlan near Caernarfon. It has a $7\frac{1}{4}$-inch gauge, has only one locomotive, and its owner has built the rolling stock, laid the track, maintains everything, sells the tickets, drives the train and answers inquiries. It is a living for one man who does his own thing.

Then there are major operations like the Festiniog Railway, also in North Wales, which operates with a large full-time staff. Vacancies do arise from time to time and lead to a totally absorbing (though not financially very rewarding) way of life. The best way in is to go volunteering regularly.

Lines like the Festiniog have of course to be totally professional in their approach to railroading. Having received much welcome help from big brother in the past, they were able to reciprocate recently by fitting oil-burning equipment to British Rail's last three steam locomotives, those that take happy crowds up the really beautiful and afforested Cwm Rheidol from Aberystwyth to Devil's Bridge. Now that oil-burners are used the valley can stay beautiful even in dry summers!

Another example of B.R. not being too proud to learn from the small 'daisy-picking' lines concerns the oldest purely pleasure railway in Britain. This is the Ravenglass & Eskdale, situated near the coast on the western edge of the Lake District. It was laid in 1916 on the abandoned roadbed of an old mineral line and it pioneered the use of a narrow gauge as slim as 15 inches for a public railway several miles in length. Sixty-five years later the 'Eskdale' is more popular than ever, and has scads of steam and diesel trains controlled by a sophisticated radio despatching system. This works so well and is so economic that British Rail is showing an interest in using it for serious railroading, and a proposal has been made to introduce the system on the East Suffolk line between Ipswich and Lowestoft.

Perhaps this chapter has been a little more serious than the others; the reason is that, instead of pointing out pleasurable and less serious aspects of things which are wholly serious, we have had to think about the serious aspects of lines that are wholly for pleasure. Taking this a little further, all the pleasure railways (like everything else in creation) have a fight for survival on their hands; almost without exception this takes the form of a continuing financial struggle. So far it is a pleasure to report that those who have lost the battle can be counted on the fingers of one hand.

22 · PRESERVING A STEAM LOCOMOTIVE

Electrify, they say, and gone, gone is the
Wonder and Romance of the Iron Road.

ROWLAND EMETT,
caption to cartoon in *Punch*

With the end of steam came preservation. The problems and
pleasures encountered by people who sought not exactly to halt
the march of progress, but at least (mixing one's metaphors) to
save something from the wreck, were fairly devastating ones.
The stories of those who tried to preserve famous locomotives
have often been told, but ones which concerned less glamorous
but (whisper it quietly) more reliable and useful machines
equally well illustrate what went on behind the scenes in these
ventures. Very vivid still in your author's mind is his involvement with the excellent L.M.S. No. 5428 (B.R. No. 45428).

The story of Cinderella has never lacked appeal; in the
locomotive world a parallel is the legendary 'Black Five' 4–6–0s
of the London Midland & Scottish Railway, 842 of which were
built between 1934 and 1949. Should a tired 'Princess' or
'Duchess' come limping into Carnforth or Carlisle with the
'Royal Scot' express, there was always a lively if shabby 'Black
Five' to replace its grander (but not, please, uglier) sister. Soon
enough the substitute would be on its way and prove to be a
wholly adequate replacement, easily capable of speeds up to 90
mph and able to produce the steam equivalent of as much coal
as a single fireman could shovel. As we have seen, north of

Perth, on the Highland line, where nothing heavier was permitted, it was a case of 'Black Five Rule O.K.' Their monumental labours both in pairs and singly on that heavily graded railway and elsewhere seemed in 1967 to your author to deserve more than one sole example whose intended fate was to be stuffed and mounted in the Clapham Transport Museum. The acquisition of one turned out to be an amazing real-life edition of the movie *Titfield Thunderbolt*.

A friend called Geoffrey Drury had then recently become the fifth private citizen in Britain to own a full-size private steam locomotive – 'joining the Mugs' Club', a mutual friend (the No. 6 private owner) called it. Geoffrey's involvement with London & North Eastern streamline 4–6–2 *Bittern*, though, was far from being a mug's game. He was running long-distance rail tours at a profit and, more important, battling with the enormous bits and pieces of his 150-ton toy was a solace for him at a time when, for private reasons, he needed one. There was fun, too, on one dark Sunday night when bringing a train load of rail-fans back from Edinburgh to York. It was suddenly realized that the bowler-hatted, black-mackintoshed gentleman who had introduced himself as a Scottish Region locomotive inspector at Edinburgh and got on the engine was in fact an impostor. They managed to stop the train in wild country above Cockburnspath, Geoffrey turned the stowaway off the engine and they steamed off into the night. There wasn't a light for miles!

The next problem was to choose a 'Black Five' and an interview with the District Motive Power Superintendent at Leeds followed. A plethora of steam locomotive plates on the wall of his office gave one confidence of his support. 'There is no problem, Mr Hollingsworth,' says Tommy Greaves, 'I'll have any Black Five in the country still running brought to Leeds and withdrawn for you.' But we soon realized that, like a conjuror forcing a card, the wide choice was more apparent than real, and the one we were eventually to have (and never regretted) was the Superintendent's pet No. 45428.

As one half of the partnership knew the procedure, the sale was arranged quickly at what seems now an amazing price of £2,643, and so early in 1968 we had our own loco. It was so hard to believe that we used to visit Holbeck Shed, Leeds, just to make sure the whole thing was not just a wonderful dream. As nice as having the loco, or nicer, was the kind treatment, help and advice we got from the shed staff at all levels. The depot was just then closing to steam, and lockers, stores and private hoards full of tools and spares were ransacked for us. But two things were apparent. First, that steam had been maintained in conditions so bad and with equipment so primitive that it was amazing that it was ever done at all. A superbly equipped new diesel repair shop next door showed what an unfair advantage diesel power had to be given in order to conquer steam. The second thing that became apparent to us and this time with horror was the enormous difficulty we were going to have as amateurs to keep this 100-ton mass of machinery in working order. The problem of finding a home now arose, as B.R. from on high had laid it down that no private owner could rent accommodation on B.R.'s system. After some searching, a berth was found at the then recently set-up museum depot at Tyseley, Birmingham. There then followed the best railway day anyone could wish for in a dozen lifetimes. Driving one's own steam locomotive down through the heart of England (under the strict supervision of the assigned crew, one hastens to add) was unbelievably satisfactory. Her ladyship behaved beautifully, the day was fine and all went well.

At Tyseley, B.R. No. 45428 got a professional repaint, arranged through the kindness of Patrick Whitehouse, founder of Tyseley, to emerge as L.M.S. No. 5428. And while the difficulties and problems of keeping her running still seemed daunting, at least we were amongst kindred spirits facing the same troubles.

Another red-letter day interlude was the naming. 'Black Fives', by dint of their designer having been second-in-command of the G.W.R. locomotive department, are directly descended from a class of locomotive of the old Great Western Railway named after saints. So we wanted a railway saint and the nearest we could get to that was the late Eric Treacy, Bishop of Wakefield, prince of railway photographers and then, by most reckonings, the No. 1 railway enthusiast of the world. The great man's permission was eagerly given, someone who had just produced the Standard Ministry of Works Dragon for the Prince of Wales' investiture designed a beautiful name plate complete with bishop's mitre and soon enough the great day of the naming dawned. The owners were about long before, however, for it takes some seven hours to raise steam on a full-size loco. Because one bishop cannot officiate in the territory of another it was a case of two for the price of one, as fortunately (and traditionally) the Bishop of Birmingham was also a railway enthusiast. The only fly in the ointment for the owner was having to make a speech in the company of two of the finest public speakers of the day. Eric Treacy said afterwards, 'I can say what I like about religion and no one takes any notice, but if I said the Great Western was a rotten railway I'd get fifty letters in the morning.'

Later, 5428 went to work on the North Yorkshire Moors Railway, where she worked until 1976. Since then she has been out of service, awaiting her turn for boiler overhaul. The cost of these, now far outside what is possible for a private individual, is being met by the North Yorkshire Moors Historical Railway Trust under agreement; so with any luck by the time this book is in print this wonderful machine will once again delight her owners and fans, pulling trains on the heavy gradients of her home line.

Perhaps you might look down on this rather timid approach to locomotive preservation, but at least 5428 is still in the hands of the original owners, whose fortunes (such as they are) have not received too serious a dent as a result of buying a steam locomotive. In stark contrast is the bold enterprise of Alan

Pegler in first buying one of Britain's most famous locomotives, the 4–6–2 *Flying Scotsman*, then finding the money for a major overhaul and after that running her over the length and breadth of Britain on dozens of special trains. The end came when in 1972 he took the engine and an exhibition train to Canada at the start of a tour of North America.

It may have been quite something to take one's own loco-motive over Shap, Dainton, Ais Gill and Cockburnspath summits, but it was something else again to ride her over the Atchison, Topeka & Santa Fe Railroad, or down the Western Pacific's Feather River Canyon line. Alas, steam railway engines have not the same draw for the public at large in the U.S.A. Federal regulations did not permit the carriage of fare-paying passengers on the main lines. So by 1973, *Flying Scotsman* was on the Embarcadero in San Francisco, giving up-and-down rides to visitors to the famous Fisherman's Wharf.

The financial situation was such that those who ran her had to wait until the first passengers turned up before buying their breakfast. In the end the engine's owner was declared bankrupt and *Flying Scotsman* herself impounded, to be rescued a year later by Bill McAlpine, who formed Flying Scotsman Enter-prises Ltd for the purpose.

All this is in aid of telling you that this is the one railway pleasure to which this book is not intended to attract you. The days are now gone by when private individuals can do these things; it now needs large groups or companies. There have in fact been no shortage of takers – *Eric Treacy* was bought in order to have *one* potential working 'Black Five' left in the world – and now there are fifteen of this type amongst some 250 main-line steam locomotives preserved in Britain alone. In fact, there has even been a debate in parliament on the subject, Robert Adey, M.P., raising the matter on the adjournment.

23 · NEW TRAINS

———

The Railway NOW is in progress. I am their
Engineer to the finest work in England – a hand-
some salary – £2,000 a year – on excellent terms
with my Directors and all going smoothly, but
what a fight we have had – and how near defeat
– and what a ruinous defeat it would have been.

ISAMBARD KINGDOM BRUNEL,
Journal, Christmas 1835

Perhaps the pleasantest thing about writing a book on the
pleasures of railways is that even today there are new trains
and railways to enjoy. New ones are being built for all sorts of
reasons. Take China for example:

	China	Britain
Population	827 million	56 million
Land area (sq. miles)	3,700,000	93,000
Miles of railway	33,900	12,200
Miles of railway per million of population	40	218
Miles of railway per 1,000 sq. miles	9	130

If you consider the arithmetic, it is small wonder that in
China new railway is being opened at the rate of 500 km per
year, while in Britain there is a definite feeling that we still
have too much, especially amongst those who have to find the
money to keep B.R.'s present network in being.

The new lines in China are consequently far from being

specialized transport links – which is the form new railways take in most of the rest of the weold – and accordingly very pleasurable to the railway enthusiast who likes to see railways taking over from rather than being superseded by other forms of common carrier. On a recent rail tour of China it was a surprise on one overnight trip for our train to set off down a line which went in the right direction but was shown on the map to be a cul-de-sac. Soon enough the express with a new 2–10–2 at its head was pounding its way over a brand-new heavily engineered line through the mountains. *A 1980s' steam locomotive running on a 1980s' railway!*

It need hardly be said that we were on our way to see a sight unparalleled elsewhere in the world today – the factory at Datong in Shansi province, where these iron horses are being mass-produced to the tune of 300 per annum. Of course, for a railway which has a 10 per cent annual increase in traffic and 8,000 steam locomotives in service, even this high rate of building steam power is far from being enough to maintain the *status quo vis à vis* diesels and electrics.

A major treat which we hope is in store for railway lovers in a few years' time is a ride across the roof of the world, crossing passes higher than those in the Andes, from Peking to the now not quite so forbidden city of Lhasa. It is difficult to imagine that it will be a steam ride, although the only photograph seen of the 400 miles of new line already in use out of the 1,400 new miles needed altogether for this railway does show steam haulage.

Elsewhere, few general-purpose railways are being built. Specialized lines are the order of the day and four quite distinct kinds can be found. First, the high-speed long-distance passenger lines which are going to bring back a flood of customers to rail travel. Second, and equally exciting, are the new mass mineral movers, of which many are being built around the world. Third, new metros to handle the mass passenger transit needs of cities. Last (and in this case least), a fair number but a minute mileage of new pleasure railways coming into service each year.

In addition, there are lines which, although new, are more in the nature of links or deviations. The National Coal Board intends to open a vast mine near Selby in Yorkshire; subsidence would reduce the proud 125-mph east-coast main line above it to tramway status, so British Rail insists on a diversion (now under construction) to avoid not only the mine but sharp curves and a swing bridge at Selby. In strong contrast, the Festiniog Railway (by two weeks the oldest railway company in the world still operating trains) needed to divert its line over a section which was flooded by a hydro-electric scheme. Volunteers set to and in thirteen years built a deviation which included a 300-yard tunnel and the only railway spiral in Britain. Dare we mention the two thirty-mile-plus tunnel schemes: the Seikan Tunnel connecting the Japanese islands of Honshu and Hokkaido, which is under way but has financial troubles; and our own Channel Tunnel, whose construction does at last seem to have a fair chance of proceeding?

Returning to specialist railways, without doubt easily the most exciting amongst the various new high-speed projects now in progress is in France. The new railway from Paris to Lyons, where *haute cuisine* has been traded for high speed, has already been mentioned. Railway-lovers are perhaps grateful that the former is not going to be there to distract them from the very keen pleasure of travelling over a brand new railway in a brand new train, both of them of new and brilliant concept. The problem of selling the idea of building high-speed railways lies in the vast cost of making them straight enough in an undulating countryside. It took French brilliance to spot that, if all the trains were new and purpose-built, gradients could be traded off for straightness; the result is a Roman road of a railway marching direct across the Burgundian countryside but going over the hills and not through them. In one place and for the first time in the history of the world there has to be a speed restriction over the top of a hump, at a place where two opposing 1 in 28½ gradients meet; no railway enthusiast worth his salt can wait to sample that. And even in the short interval between finishing Chapter 14 and writing this one, a new record speed of 238 mph for a train running on a public railway has been achieved during trial running on a completed section of this new line. These French developments have been characterized by what is very much an 'on time' performance in relation to the originally announced timetable.

In sad contrast is British Rail's Advanced Passenger Train, the development of which has been dogged by a series of delays. It is a remarkable concept in that the A.P.T. was designed to do the very high speed of 150 mph and, by tilting the bodies of the cars, go comfortably at this speed round curves that otherwise would necessitate a reduction to 100 mph or so. Hence super-fast schedules without new railways. The tragedy lies in the fact that even though the new train went into service in 1981, eight years behind the originally announced date, the fact that the maximum speed has had to be reduced means that there is little advantage in operating it on the only line on which it can work, the A.P.T. being now electrically driven. There is just a suspicion that what is really wanted is an electric version of the H.S.T. 125 train to take over services between London and Glasgow and a 100- or even 80-mph diesel-driven version of the A.P.T. to take over services on lesser lines which are infested with speed restriction of the 40–50–60-mph kind. Even so, railway-lovers are looking forward with the keenest pleasure to experiencing A.P.T. tilting on those few curves between Euston and Scotland where the tilting mechanism is of use.

Equally sad is the state of play on the proposed German new high-speed network and on the extensions of the now no longer new Japanese Shin Kansen 'bullet train' lines. Escalating financial problems for the railways as a whole in both these countries have eaten into funds which otherwise might have been available. Possibly this pause might be the moment to rethink the schemes on the 'Roman road' principle, using straight or barely curved alignments and steep gradients.

It is hardly more than a generation or so ago that the start of a mining enterprise meant a couple of partners ('pardners' was the term used if the movies are to be believed) joining forces in order to buy a pick, a shovel, a wheelbarrow and a mule. When a few years ago the Hammersley Iron Company decided to mine some 20 to 40 million tons of iron ore annually in the almost uninhabited top left-hand corner of Australia, things were different. It meant a brand new 240-mile heavy-duty high-iron railway line from the mining area at Mount Tom Price to the new port at Dampier; and a traction set-up that would enable mile-long trains of 23,000 gross tons to be worked by groups of the largest obtainable diesel locomotives running in multiple. Even the most unforgiving steam enthusiast could, like the ranks of Tuscany, 'scarce forebear to cheer' at such heroic doings, especially if one adds the fact that the company bought one of the world's most famous steam locomotives, the ex-Great Western Railway No. 4079 *Pendennis Castle*, as something to amuse the staff in off-duty moments! Opportunities sometimes occur to ride behind 'Pen' when she is run. There is even talk of an attempt to break the Australian speed record for steam traction on this freight-only line.

Others amongst these mineral movers even have a vestigial passenger service which in a few cases actually reaches Cook's *Overseas Timetable*. The Quebec, North Shore & Labrador, which is reached by an all-day bus ride down the north bank of the St Lawrence River from Quebec and runs a twice-a-week train from the port of Sept Îles to the mining area 360 miles inland at Schafferville, even has dining-car and motor-rail service. In West Africa, the Republic of Mauritania's sole rail service, in a country twice the size of France, is on the 400-mile National Mining Company's line from Nouadhibou to Zouerate. Other examples could be cited, but a journey on either of these two would put a railway enthusiast into the elite class.

The southernmost railway in the world is a newish coal-hauling line in Argentina not far from Cape Horn, a part of the world where what we regard as gale-force winds are considered to be almost a flat calm. The authorities can, it seems, be persuaded to attach an ancient coach to one of the trains, which are all pulled by 2–10–2 steam locomotives. These are the most modern in the world in that their fires burn the coal in a new manner almost like a gas works. Apart from super-heating, it is the only fundamental change ever successfully carried out on the steam locomotive since the Stephensons' day.

Exhaust steam is introduced into the firebed, while the air needed for combustion, instead of coming in through the firebed, is introduced above it through apertures in the side of the boiler. Black smoke and the throwing of sparks and cinders is reduced while efficiency is greatly improved. The idea has recently been tried out in South Africa. Before recent events this Rio Gallegos line, hundreds of miles from the nearest hotel, became a place of pilgrimage for the worshipper of steam.

New metros have been coming in thick and fast the world over, except in this the country of their birth, where progress has been very slow. London got the world's first Metropolitan Railway in 1864, but the second English city had to wait until 1980, when the first section of Newcastle-upon-Tyne's Metro was opened. Since Glasgow's Underground has also had new trains maybe things are now changing 'down below' even in Britain. So far as railway lovers are concerned, in a country where trains look very much the same from Penzance to Aberdeen, Holyhead to Norwich or Weymouth to Thurso, the three metros offer very refreshing variety in appearance, technology and concept.

Also new is an underground loop in Liverpool for B.R. trains, and back into the fold has come the Great Northern & City tube in London. This runs from Finsbury Park to Moorgate and was built many years ago to be ready for the electrification of the Great Northern Railway's suburban services. This arrived slightly late ('British Rail apologize for the inconvenience caused to passengers') and during the intervening seventy years London Transport and its predecessors operated a shuttle service, latterly of life-expired tube trains, which looked a little lost in the big tubes designed for the main-line stock. Before the changeover the now refurbished intermediate stations looked neglected in the manner of rented property, but sinister indeed were the staircases leading out of them which, by a quirk of the design, led *downwards*. Worrying.

Finally, returning to frivolity after this macabre note, we find that new pleasure railways are coming in steadily. Even in the time between writing and typing this book, the railway-lovers' world will be the richer for yet another. It is still a world where individuals and small groups are able to do their own thing and both gain and give great pleasure thereby. Jim Haylock's Tuck-tonia Railway at Christchurch, Dorset, at the moment the newest railway in the world, has many delightful features. Although the gauge is only $7\frac{1}{4}$ inches, the trains are not models – model railways are a whole world of railway pleasure outside the scope of this book – but designed to do a transport job in their own right. The locomotives, *Talos*, *Medea* and *Tinkerbell*, have to be got into to drive – even 6 foot 5 inch drivers can (just) insert themselves and manage comfortably; the same goes for the de luxe closed passenger carriages. Approximately one hundred years ago a certain Sir Arthur Percival Heywood startled his contemporaries by building both a sleeping car and a dining car for the 15-inch gauge. Perhaps one day soon we shall see sleepers and diners on even narrower tracks.

24 · THE END OF THE LINE

Not only have we no solution – but we are
part of the problem.

ANON. (*seen on a blackboard in the back rooms
of the Southern Pacific Railway, U.S.A.*)

The end of the line means more pleasures for the railway
enthusiast, even if somewhat melancholy ones. First, there are
the sad pleasures of the funerals to be enjoyed. With luck the
last rites can be celebrated several times. Occasion No. 1 is
when a railway leaves local ownership and becomes part of some
larger conglomeration. In Britain forty years ago the initials
G.W.R., S.R. and L.N.E.R. were universally known. A certain
family, friends of the writer long ago, had a giant sofa downstairs
and, although none of them were railway enthusiasts, they called
it L.M.S. – the letters standing not for London, Midland &
Scottish but for Love Made Simple! But I'm afraid the joke is
lost on both the children and the grandchildren (as you might
expect, numerous) of the boys and girls who first explored
the possibilities of passion with the aid of L.M.S.

In their turn, previous generations in Britain had mourned
the loss of such names as Manchester, Sheffield & Lincoln-
shire ('Money Sunk & Lost) and its successor the Great
Central ('Gone Completely'), the London Chatham and Dover
('London, Smashem and Turnover') the Caledonian ('The
Caley'), The London, Brighton & South Coast ('The Brighton')

and many others. To most, the losses were felt as keenly as those of personal friends.

In America the process is still continuing. There the faithful lament the way in which such great railroads as Baltimore & Ohio ('The B&O is the Way to Go'), Chicago, Burlington & Quincy ('Everywhere West'), Lehigh Valley ('Route of the Black Diamond'), Northern Pacific ('Main Street of the North West'), Pennsylvania ('The Pennsy') and the Wabash ('Follow the Flag') – to name just a few – have rolled on into the oblivion of such great corporations as Chessie System, Burlington Northern and Conrail.

After amalgamation and nationalization have taken their toll the extinction of passenger service is the next step. The rail-fan element can mark this by a pleasurably sad excursion to travel the trains on the last day. But this is not always the end: a year or two later there often arises the possibility of chartering special trains to explore what will have become a streak of rust leading out into the unknown. Such trains have everything. First, there is the joy of battle with the administration, who are understandably reluctant to upgrade temporarily a freight line to passenger standards. Second, of course, travellers on these excursions in consequence feel like privileged beings – sometimes whole villages turn out to greet them as if they were royalty – while at the same time there is the sense of being explorers in an unknown land. This is an old facet of the Great Railway Game and even forty years ago there were hundreds of miles of freight-only branches in Britain. Very few of them failed to get visited by trains carrying railway enthusiasts, even if sometimes they had to travel in open freight wagons, having previously signed their lives away on legal indemnities against any claim for damages should an accident occur.

Finally, of course, the scrap-men arrive and take the metals away. Demolition trains are fascinating, of course, but with typical lack of consideration they tend to run during the working week rather than at weekends, when they could more easily be enjoyed by the lovers of strange railway happenings. Once that is done, nature takes charge of what have now become the amazing networks of overgrown trails of vanished lines, sometimes marked tantalizingly on maps as 'Tk of Old Rly'. It is a fairly wide field, with perhaps 50,000 miles of abandoned grades in the U.S.A., over 10,000 in Britain, nearer 20,000 in France and many miles elsewhere. At a conservative ten miles a day one could spend a happy and healthy half-century of leisure time exploring them.

The earliest known closure is that of the Newmarket and Chesterford Railway, between Chesterford and Six Mile Bottom, completed in 1846 and abandoned in 1851, when the Eastern Counties Railway decided to make passengers for the racehorse capital of the world travel via, and change at, Cambridge. The earthworks and even some artifacts of this line still, 130 years later, look as if a minor wash and brush-up would ready them for track laying. This wide world beyond the end of the line in Britain has recently been set down in John Ransom's definitive *British Railway Archeology* (Windmill Press, 1981).

So, in saying that there is much beyond the end of the line, we come finally to the last buffer stops in this journey through the pleasures which railways offer. If it is a journey you have never tried, it is the author's hope it will inspire you to set out; while, if you have already been some of the way, perhaps one or two new ways in which pleasure can be extracted from the world's million miles of iron road will suggest themselves.

INDEX

MORE ABOUT PENGUINS, PELICANS
AND PUFFINS

For further information about books available from Penguins please write to Dept EP, Penguin Books Ltd, Harmondsworth, Middlesex UB7 0DA.

In the U.S.A.: For a complete list of books available from Penguins in the United States write to Dept DG, Penguin Books, 299 Murray Hill Parkway, East Rutherford, New Jersey 07073.

In Canada: For a complete list of books available from Penguins in Canada write to Penguin Books Canada Ltd, 2801 John Street, Markham, Ontario L3R 1B4.

In Australia: For a complete list of books available from Penguins in Australia write to the Marketing Department, Penguin Books Australia Ltd, P.O. Box 257, Ringwood, Victoria 3134.

In New Zealand: For a complete list of books available from Penguins in New Zealand write to the Marketing Department, Penguin Books (N.Z.) Ltd, P.O. Box 4019, Auckland 10.

In India: For a complete list of books available from Penguins in India write to Penguin Overseas Ltd, 706 Eros Apartments, 56 Nehru Place, New Delhi 110019.

Also by Brian Hollingsworth

HOW TO DRIVE A STEAM LOCOMOTIVE

For steam enthusiasts, railway buffs and for everyone who has ever dreamed of being up in the cab of a locomotive . . .

The engine and how it works – from the controls and steam power to pistons, rods and valves.

Out on the line – from headlights and working timetables to speed restrictions and emergency stops.

Getting to drive a loco yourself – from miniature railways and building your own to your local live-steam club.

'Well-written, well-illustrated . . . It will instruct, interest, please and amuse many would-be engine drivers as well as many who no longer aspire to such heights, not to say some who have actually done the job' – *Railway Magazine*

'Delightful and informative . . . anyone who has even the faintest of interest in the steam locomotive should obtain a copy, read it and enjoy it' – *Railway Modeller*

'Highly original . . . should serve to whet the appetite of every enthusiast who has ever dreamed of riding the footplate' – *Transport Review*

THE GREAT RAILWAY BAZAAR

Fired by a fascination with trains that stemmed from childhood, Paul Theroux set out one day with the intention of boarding every train that chugged into view from Victoria Station in London to Tokyo Central, and to come back again via the Trans-Siberian Express.

'In the fine old tradition of purposeless travel for fun and adventure . . . compulsive reading' – Graham Greene

'One of the most entertaining books I have read in a long time . . . superb comic detail' – Angus Wilson in the *Observer*

'More than a rich and original entertainment. His people, places and asides will stay a long time jostling in the mind of the reader' – V. S. Pritchett in the *New Statesman*

THE OLD PATAGONIAN EXPRESS

'One of the most entrancing travel books written in our time' – C. P. Snow in the *Financial Times*

'I studied my maps and there appeared to be a continuous track from my house in Medford to the Great Plateau of Patagonia in southern Argentina. There, in the town of Esquel, one ran out of railways.'

From blizzard-stricken Boston to arid Patagonia; travelling by luxury express and squalid local trucks; sweating and shivering by turns as the temperature and altitude shot up and down; thrown in with the appalling Mr Thornberry in Limon and reading nightly to the blind writer, Borges, in Buenos Aires; Paul Theroux's vivid pen clearly evokes the contrasts of a journey 'to the end of the line'.

'Fascinating, beautifully written . . . a vivid travelogue described with the sensitive, richly observant pen of a born writer' – *Sunday Express*

ORIENT EXPRESS
E. H. Cookridge

A president of France fell off it. An American spy was pushed off it. A Spanish duchess was rescued from her manic bridegroom on it. Hitchcock filmed it. Agatha Christie, Graham Greene and Ian Fleming wrote bestsellers about it . . .

The very name of the Orient Express, with its silk and marble fittings, is redolent with fame and riches, spies and diplomats and the luxury and romance of the mysterious East. And on this unique train, immortalized here by E. H. Cookridge, truth was very often stranger than fiction.

'A splendid book' – Arthur Marshall in the *New Statesman*

'Unfailingly readable' – *New York Times Book Review*

SLOW BOATS TO CHINA
Gavin Young

Ancient steamer in the Aegean, cargo dhow to Karachi, Filipino kumpit through the pirate-infested Sulu Sea . . .

It needed twenty-three agreeably ill-assorted vessels and seven months to transport Gavin Young by slow boat from Piraeus to Canton – seven months crowded with adventure, excitement and colour. His account of a fantasy come true memorably distils the people, places, smells, conversations, ships and history of the places he encountered in a quite exceptional book.

'An unusual and fascinating book' – Hammond Innes in the *Guardian*

'Storms, fleas, pirates, bad food and bureaucrats . . . Mr Young suffered what he did to entertain us' – Anthony Burgess in the *Observer*

PENGUIN TRAVEL LIBRARY

A selection

Passages from Arabia Deserta

C. M. DOUGHTY

Selected by Edward Garnett

Eccentric, redolent with sharply observed life, anecdote, local colour and telling detail, *Arabia Deserta* is not only a Victorian traveller's interpretation of a mysterious – and largely unfathomed – Orient, but also a daring experiment in the use of language at its richest.

'A book so majestic, so vital, of such incomparable beauty of thought, of observation, and of diction as to occupy a place apart' – *Observer*

One's Company

PETER FLEMING

Packed with classic incidents – brake-failure on the Trans-Siberian Express, the Eton Boating Song singing lesson in Manchuria – *One's Company* is Peter Fleming's account of his journey to China as Special Correspondent to *The Times* in 1933.

'Original and impressive ... As a journalist he is modernity itself; as a traveller he has about him an Elizabethan aroma, being both cruel and amused' – Harold Nicolson in the *Daily Telegraph*

Africa Dances

GEOFFREY GORER

Describing his travels through French West Africa, Senegal, French Guinea, the Ivory Coast, Dahomey, the Gold Coast and Nigeria, Geoffrey Gorer's marvellous book vividly recreates an Africa on the point of transition.

'He has made one of the most singular journeys of modern times ... There are no reservations in this astonishing book. Sex, religion, politics, the negro conception of life contrasted with the white man's, the place of fetish and magic, wrestling, dancing and marriage ... The result is a book I could not put down' – *Daily Telegraph*